PLUMAS COUNTY

HISTORY OF THE FEATHER RIVER REGION

The Feather River was originally named "El Rio de las Plumas" in 1821 by Spanish explorer Luis Antonio Argüello for the multitude of waterfowl seen upon its waters. About 1850 it was anglicized to "Feather River."

THE
MAKING OF AMERICA
SERIES

PLUMAS COUNTY
HISTORY OF THE FEATHER RIVER REGION

JIM YOUNG

EDITED BY
PLUMAS COUNTY MUSEUM ASSOCIATION

ARCADIA
PUBLISHING

Published by Arcadia Publishing
Charleston SC, Chicago IL, Portsmouth NH, San Francisco CA

For all general information contact Arcadia Publishing at:
Telephone 843-853-2070
Fax 843-853-0044
E-Mail sales@arcadiapublishing.com
For customer service and orders:
Toll-Free 1-888-313-2665

Visit us on the Internet at www.arcadiapublishing.com

Front cover: *A family picnic. Quincy resident Abby Schneider (seated, second from left in straw hat) gathered with friends and family for a summer picnic in the late 1890s. Her brother Ed Huskinson was behind a tree pouring beer.*

CONTENTS

FOREWORD

It has been fully 120 years since Fariss and Smith released their monumental work *The Illustrated History of Plumas, Lassen & Sierra Counties*. Time has marched inexorably along and finally, approaching the eve of Plumas County's 150th birthday in 2004, the long-awaited and sorely needed comprehensive history of Plumas County and the Feather River region has been written. Mr. Jim Young has devoted many years to combing through records, diaries, newspapers, and other sources in libraries and museums all over Plumas County and the state of California, in addition to interviewing residents, to bring to light the events, people, and stories that have made Plumas County what it is today. Over 100 historic photographs portraying faces, places, and events in Plumas County amply augment his text. Mr. Young has touched on just about every aspect of Plumas County from its native Maidu Native Americans, the gold rush, agricultural and timber heritage, and railroading days, through the various communities that were founded as a result of those activities. There are accounts of personal triumph and tragedy, as well as statistics related to industry.

Unfortunately, due to size constraints, some of Mr. Young's hard-gleaned information had to fall to the "cutting room" floor. This information is not lost, however; it will be retained in the Plumas County Museum's archives for researchers to access if the need arises. There are some subjects—for example, longboard skiing—that are only touched on lightly since detailed books are already available on those subjects. Within the pages of this book, Mr. Young has taken the myriad facts and information he has harvested on Plumas County and winnowed them into a narrative that will inform and intrigue you, the reader.

~Scott J. Lawson
Director, Plumas County Museum

ACKNOWLEDGMENTS

My sincere thanks to the following for their help on this project: Linda Brennan, Margaret Cooke, Don Johns, Norman Lamb, Scott Lawson, Belle Penland, Plumas County Historical Society, Plumas County Library, Plumas County Museum and its volunteers, Barbara Pricer, Judge Al Thieler, Sally Trombly, Evelyn Whisman, Judy Wright, and my wife Janice Young.

Posthumous acknowledgements are in order for the following people for their contributions to this book: Jim Boynton, Orville Brown, Bob Cooke, Billie Hogan Gronvold, Helen Lawry, and Bill Penland. I apologize for anyone I may have missed, but please be assured your input was invaluable.

~Jim Young
Quincy, California, 2002

1. MAIDU: NATIVE PEOPLE OF PLUMAS COUNTY

The Mountain Maidu have lived in Plumas County for the past 1,000 years or more. Their lifestyle revolved around an almost constant quest of gathering, hunting, and fishing. No other activity involved as much time as acquisition of food.

In the beginning, according to the Maidu, there was only the ocean. The world was flat and one lonely turtle was floating upon the great blue sea. The Creator descended from the sky and sat with Turtle. When Turtle expressed a desire for land, the Creator told him to dive to the ocean's bottom and return with some mud. The Creator and Turtle then laid the mud on the sea's surface. Upon the word of the Creator, the mud expanded and the landmass of earth was created. The Creator then called upon the Sun and the Moon to travel over the skies and create day and night. He next created the stars, birds, animals, and trees, including oak trees with acorns for food.

To ensure stability of the new landmass, the Creator stretched five ropes to anchor the earth as it floated on the ocean. The ropes stretched to the north, south, east, west, and northwest. These directions became the basis for Maidu orientation and five became the tribal sacred number—on many of their beautiful baskets, designs of five zigzags or stripes dominate the ornamentation. Coyote, the trickster, sometimes pulled on an earth-anchoring rope and created earthquakes. He made the mountains and also changed dwellings and sweathouses into stone.

Next, man was created, known as Kuksu, and woman, named Morning Star Woman. Children were born and Kuksu taught them how to hunt and fish, dance, and hold festivals, and he taught them their laws. As the population increased, Kuksu sent the people to different parts of the world. One of the groups of Maidu sailed in a canoe until they ran aground near Keddie Peak, north of Greenville. The mountain is known today by residents as "Indian Head."

The Maidu were not a single large tribe, but rather three smaller ones. The Maidu had no known tribal name by which they called themselves. In the Maidu language, *Maidu* basically means "Man" or "People." The Maidu as a people lived in a 150-mile north-south zone from Chico to Sacramento, and east-west from the Sacramento River to the top of the Sierra Nevada. The three divisions had closely related dialects, yet with enough differences to hinder precise communication. But the Maidu, like other tribes, were able to also communicate by signs. Pre–gold rush data indicates that the three groups were dispersed as follows:

> MOUNTAIN MAIDU: 2,000 to 3,000 people. Located in Plumas County and the Susanville area.
>
> KONKOW MAIDU: 3,000 to 4,000 people. Located in the Sacramento Valley from Chico to the Sutter Buttes north of Marysville and the adjoining Sierra Nevada foothills east to Bucks Lake in Plumas County.
>
> NISENAN MAIDU: 9,000 to 12,000 people. Located from Marysville to Sacramento and from the Sacramento River eastward to the top of the Sierra Nevada.

A familiar face around Taylorsville in 1900, Molly created many beautiful and serviceable baskets. She is shown here on a Taylorsville porch with an example of her work.

Maidu babies Heinie and Fritzie are snug in their "teutums" or baby carriers made of willow and leather. These young fellows lived at Big Bar, now Pulga, on the North Fork Feather River about 1911.

The Mountain Maidu had no single tribal chief. The headman was chosen by unanimous consent through the aid of a shaman who conveyed the choices of the spirits to the people. Leaders were required to possess wisdom, maturity, wealth, generosity, leadership, and popularity. The tribe was made up of approximately 12 tribelets of 100 to 500 people, each having its own leader. Each tribelet had a number of villages in the valleys. One tribelet of several hundred Maidu lived in Big Meadows, with a smaller tribelet in nearby Butt Valley. Probably the largest tribelet lived in Indian Valley. Three large villages existed in the Taylorsville area and another in Genesee Valley.

American Valley had 150 to 250 Maidu, living in four to six villages scattered along its southern facing slopes. Additional tribelets lived in Meadow Valley, Mohawk Valley, and Sierra Valley.

The Maidu believed the land, water, trees, and air were communal property. Occasionally, food acquisition raids or kidnapping of women occurred. Konkow Maidu from the Sacramento Valley would sometimes kidnap younger Mountain Maidu women of childbearing age and sometimes children were captured for adoption. The Mountain Maidu would often retaliate and invade Konkow lands.

Occasionally, killings occurred during the kidnappings. Marie Potts, a respected twentieth-century Maidu author, tells about the Yahi from the Mill Creek region raiding, killing, and kidnapping Maidu in Big Meadows. Another respected Maidu elder, Tom Epperson, agreed with her. An 1866 newspaper reported a Yana raid from Tehama County on the Indian Valley Maidu, killing four people. The Maidu retaliated, killing one of the Yana near Mill Creek. Shortly thereafter, the Yana returned to Big Meadows and killed another Maidu.

Ambushes were a typical method of warfare. Since there was no political or military tribal authority, warriors usually acted alone or in small groups. For protection, a waistcoat of mountain mahogany sticks woven together with willows or grapevines was used. Warfare was never carried out for territorial acquisition.

Traditional Maidu enemies were the Yahi, a subgroup of the Yana; the Washoe in eastern California; and the Pit Rivers, a subgroup of the Achamawi. The Maidu were generally on good terms with the Paiutes. On April 29, 1858, the *Plumas Argus* reported a difficulty with Pit River Indians in the Honey Lake region where, due to food shortages, the Pit Rivers encroached on Maidu lands and also stole from the settlers there. The settlers were not sure which tribe was responsible for the potato losses from their fields and, not surprisingly, the losses resulted in what has become known as the Potato War. Plumas Rangers from Quincy came to the aid of the Honey Lake settlers and Paiute Chief Winnemucca and his people tried to help, but they arrived too late to prevent hostilities.

Maidu sweathouses were large, circular semi-subterranean structures. These substantial buildings also doubled as men's work and social areas. Women were not allowed into these buildings. There was one entrance and a smoke hole in the top of the roof.

Captain Aleck and his wife Eliza posed for a local photographer in 1897. Aleck was born in the 1830s in American Valley and was the "Yup-on-im" or headman for a Maidu village in the Keddie–Goat Hill area. His wife Eliza Connet was also born in the same area in the 1830s. They had 10 children during their marriage. Aleck died in 1908, Eliza in 1921.

Sierra Valley was a boon for rabbit hunting. Hunters made a long horseshoe-shaped fence of willows and drove the rabbits into it to be clubbed to death. Deer, a prominent food source, were available until winter.

Hunters often used deer masks, made from the head and upper body of deer, as a decoy and could skillfully creep on the downwind side of their prey to get within shooting range. They would also call the deer by imitating a bawling fawn with a grass stem. Sometimes a group would gather at a game route, while others rousted and drove the game through the woods toward a fence, which slowed them down, enabling hunters to shoot them.

A significant number of grizzly and black bear existed in the area, but the hazards of hunting them could and did result in injury or death. Grizzly bears were the most dangerous and were avoided, but occasionally a daring hunter received praise by killing a mature black bear. Bears provided an abundance of meat, as well as oil and a hide for soft bedding.

Smaller game like quail, ground squirrels, and pigeons were also hunted. Pigeons were shot by bow and arrow, while swiftly-moving quail and ground squirrels were killed by a variety of methods: snares, bow and arrows, well-thrown rocks, or traps. Waterfowl were shot, or caught in nooses that were hung by a cord above the marshy bottomland or water's surface. Killing eagles was bad luck and never attempted.

Fish were an important source of food for the Maidu. Trout, carp, suckers, and eels were taken, but salmon was the preferred catch. Fishhooks were made from bird bones and the fishing line made from deer sinew or the inner bark of trees. Large nets were stretched the width of a small creek. Children and teenage boys and girls would go upstream of the net, then come jumping and shouting downstream, scaring the fish into the net.

The most lucrative season for catching salmon each year was in late September or early October, the spawning season, and it was believed that the large number swimming upstream to spawn benefited the tribe. Harley C. Flournoy, a long-time resident of Indian and Genesee Valleys said, "at the falls in Big Meadows, the Maidu caught tons and tons of salmon," and that much of the catch was smoked and dried for storage over the long winter.

Gathering was essential to the Maidu. The most important foods were acorns, berries, nuts, seeds, and roots. The Maidu also gathered grasshoppers, crickets, ants, and grubs.

Probably the most elaborate cultural activity the Maidu engaged in was the gathering and preparation of acorns, their most important staple. During the autumn, fallen acorns were gathered by village members and carried in large burden baskets to storage bins made of willow. Acorn soup and bread were the primary foodstuffs produced.

After the acorns were gathered, women used two stones to crack the acorn shells in halves, removed the meat with their fingers and teeth, and spread it on the ground to dry. Next, the dried acorn meat was placed in a rock mortar. Sometimes the mortars were holes in a large rock on the ground or often they were made from semi-portable rocks about 1 foot or so in diameter. After years of grinding acorns and seeds, the hole in the mortar increased in smoothness, depth, and width. Some mortar holes could be 1 foot or more deep. When acorns or seeds were dumped into the mortar hole, a 3- to 4-inch handheld pestle, or mano, was used to grind and pulverize the meat into fine flour. The flour was removed and spread on a bed of cedar boughs lying over sand. More boughs were placed over the meal and warm water was poured gently over it all to leach out bitter tannic acid. This process continued for several hours until the acid was removed.

When this lengthy process was completed, a fire was started a short distance away. As the fire gradually turned to coals, a large flat stone was placed on the bed of coals and a basket on the large flat stone. Flour and water were mixed in the basket to begin the acorn soup cooking process. Small hot stones were placed in the basket to help heat the soup. Stirring continued until the rocks cooled and heating ceased. The resulting thick soup was now ready to eat, hot or cold. Acorn dough was made into bread by wrapping it in leaves and placing it on coals under hot stones to bake. The high calorie value of either finished product was an essential addition to the Maidu diet.

Camas roots and Indian potatoes were leading root staples, Indian potatoes being about the size of a peanut. Both grew abundantly and were a reliable source of food in season. Epos, a wild member of the parsley family, provided carrot-like roots from Plumas meadows. They were dried and stored for winter, as were various seed crops. Wild onions, common at higher elevations, were also utilized.

In summer, most men went naked or wore only a buckskin breechcloth. Women wore a two-piece skirt covering front and back from the waist to just above their knees. The skirt, or apron, was normally of buckskin or shredded inner tree bark. If buckskin, the bottom few inches were fringed to permit freer movement. Winter garb usually consisted of an animal skin or blanket-type robe of deer skin, elk skin, or rabbit skins sewed together. This blanket was draped over one or both shoulders with the fur side in.

Deerskin moccasins that reached above the ankle were worn when hunting, traveling, or collecting wood; however, around the village, most went barefoot. In winter, grass was stuffed inside for extra warmth and deer hide gaiters, hair side in, were worn from ankle to knees.

William Tell Parker, a gold miner in Plumas County in the 1850s, described the Maidu as "dressed in their national costume which is nudity." Parker related the following from July 1851:

> This morning the (Indian) ladies repaired to the river above our dam, laid off their blankets and took a swim. They wear a piece of blanket or deer skin loosely around them and nothing underneath but a bunch of grass roots resembling a kickdry broom in front and another behind which dangle from a girdle.

Semi-subterranean wooden structures were constructed 3 to 4 feet above the ground and 2 to 3 feet below the ground. These homes were the most substantial structures made by the Mountain Maidu and provided each family with protection from rain and snow. The dirt was banked along the exterior edge to serve as a foundation for the exterior walls. A sturdy tree trunk or post forked at the top stood in the floor's center, from which poles were tied together at the top. These connected pieces were spread out and down like an umbrella and became the skeleton for the walls and roof.

Additional poles and large chunks of bark were leaned and placed over the framework. Tree moss was used as weather stripping to plug cracks in the walls. The door for entering and exiting was simply a deerskin or mat made of willows. The 10- to 16-inch smoke hole on top of the roof was covered with skins when no fire inside the house was burning.

Interior maximum height was enough to allow standing. The dirt floor of the dwelling eventually obtained a cement-like hardness through dampening and constant use. Willows, cattails, pine needles, and cedar fronds were spread about the sleeping area as a partial mattress, while deer or elk hides, bear skins, or rabbit skins sewed together served as the mattress and blanket.

For a substantial part of the warmer seasons, food acquisition became life's priority, with most residents of a village becoming seasonal nomads during these five or six months. Temporary lean-tos or thatched summer homes were quickly erected. During good food supply periods, discretionary time was available for advancing technological needs, social and cultural improvements, and religion.

Births were attended by the grandmother, an older sister, and maybe an aunt. The mother gave birth at home in a sitting position while a shaman outside would chant in a low-toned, reassuring manner to ensure a successful birth. Normally, the child was not given a name until two or three years old, being simply known as boy, girl, or baby.

For boys, there were no formal puberty traditions. Girls underwent a more important rite of passage. On the first day of menstruation, the daughter and mother went into the hills where certain traditional customs were carried out. After a few days, mother and daughter built a fire to signal the village that they were returning and ceremonial preparations should begin. Upon their return, singing and dancing around a large fire every evening was held for a week. Then the young lady had her ears pierced, and dancing and singing resumed for another two or three days.

Marriage often consisted of simply living together as marriage partners. No wedding ceremony was conducted and infidelity was rare. The average woman lived only to around 40 years of age, childbirth being the leading cause of death, while the average man lived to his 40s or 50s.

The Maidu of Indian Valley built campoodies from lumber scraps salvaged from local sawmills and cedar bark from the hills. These summer shelters were also built to take advantage of the southern exposures along the valley's edges.

The Maidu believed in a Creator and that their lifestyle was determined by spirits, as well as the physical world. It was essential to be kind and reverent to the physical world. Since each Maidu living in the physical world had a soul, they believed trees, animals, birds, and fish also had souls.

Maidu religion was a very important part of life and helped them interpret and provide answers to life's unknowns. Religion gave them the means to cope with the supernatural and life's daily occurrences. In matters of death, mourning signs exhibited by women were to cut their hair short, rub pitch and mud on their faces, and wear old dirty clothes. Men did the same only when their father died. The dead were generally buried in a fetal position facing the east with a few personal possessions, water, and food. Following a death, the deceased's home was deserted and sometimes burned, so evil spirits would not return to it.

The shaman was a doctor as well as a religious leader, and sometimes was a woman. The shaman exercised significant influence over the tribelet in religion, health, and social guidance. Shamans gained their position through inheritance, but had to undergo an intense period of instruction from older shamans to gain their knowledge in the art of curing ailments.

The shaman practiced various methods of cure, such as chanting or rubbing the afflicted part of the patient's body with salves made from plants and leaves.

This young lady found the angling still pretty good on the North Fork of the Feather River in 1915. The Maidu lived along the river at various points where fish, berries, and acorns were plentiful.

Emetics were sometimes administered, causing the patient to vomit, thus releasing bad spirits from inside the body. Suction was the primary method of cure. The Maidu believed bad spirits caused illnesses, so the shaman first located the evil spirits, then placed a hollow reed against the afflicted area and sucked through it to remove the evil spirits from the body.

Bad spirits were expelled by taking daily baths in a sweathouse for up to two hours. Hot rocks from a fire were moved inside the sweathouse and the bathers sat on boughs spread on the ground. Some participated in talk, while others intermittently sang and chanted using religious and curative lyrics. After a time, the bathers left the sweathouse and dove in a nearby stream, or during winter, rubbed their bodies with snow.

There were two types of sweathouses: small ones 6 to 8 feet in diameter were used primarily by the women and children, and large ones 50 to 60 feet in diameter were used exclusively by the men.

The large sweathouse became the most important and prominent structure of the group. Sweathouses were multi-purpose structures. Dancing was often enjoyed in the sweathouse, hence its alternate name of dance house. They were also used as a social center, or men's club, where the men would talk, make bows, arrows, and fishing nets, gamble, or sleep. Women were not allowed inside.

Maidu baskets are impressive monuments of their culture. Willow, maple, pine needles, or redbud fibers and vegetable materials such as bear grass, brake, and ferns were used to make baskets, hats, and baby cradles. Burden or gathering baskets could be completed in a few weeks or a month at most. The tightly woven, small seed or water baskets could take longer to make. All baskets were circular, but their forms and sizes varied a great deal. Typical Maidu pattern arrangement was generally diagonal and parallel.

Genesee native Frank Joseph told how his mother Freda made the beautiful Native American baskets on display at the Indian Valley Museum in Taylorsville:

> Every fall, the Indians burned off the willows and maples so that in the spring there would be tender young shoots to pick. The bark from the willow was removed immediately after picking, with a piece of flint. The maple shoots were heated over a small fire with the bark on. The shoot was quartered the full length, then worked to a uniform size and thickness. The willow was used only for the core of the basket, so it was picked in different lengths and sizes for different size baskets. The maple was woven over the core with an awl made from a piece of bone. While weaving, a pan of water was kept handy to dampen the wood frequently, to avoid cracking and splitting, and to shape the basket. If the basket is soaked for a time, it will eventually become watertight. The white and black colors are from maple wood, the white being natural and the black being dyed with oak bark. The red color is from the bark of the redbud tree. The designs are completely planned before the basket is made and all the designs have a meaning and tell a story.

17

Maidu students were taught vocational and household skills at the government-built "Indian Mission School" near Greenville. Gardening, carpentry, plumbing, cooking, and sewing were among the courses at this school from 1885 until it burned in the early 1900s.

Throughout man's history, people have been displaced for various reasons and by various means. Statistically speaking, the Mountain Maidu in Indian Valley fared significantly better overall than other California Native Americans. The approximately 500 Mountain Maidu existing in 1847 dwindled to 250 in 1900, while 100,000 total California Native Americans in 1847 were reduced to only 16,000 in 1900. During the first three to five decades of the white man's arrival, the Maidu had lost half of their tribelet members. They did not have guns or the political organization to resist. They stepped aside and watched the white man take over. They no longer had control of their own destiny.

The federal government decided Native Americans should be assimilated by going to school and learning the white man's language. The federally funded Greenville Indian School was built in 1888 to serve as a day school for Indian Valley Native Americans and a boarding school for other northern California tribesmen. The original building, a 20- by 40-foot wooden structure, burned in 1897. The new school, built in 1898, was larger, having classrooms, dormitories, a dining-social hall combination, a sewing room, and a medical dispensary, washrooms with modern plumbing, and a steam laundry. Subsequent additions included a clubhouse, gymnasium, machine shop, warehouses, garage, and barn. Beginning with 15 students and 2 teachers, by 1901 the Greenville Indian School had 78 students and 8 teachers.

Indian Valley Maidu children and parents were reasonably receptive to the school at first. The curriculum included instruction in reading and writing English and mathematics. Vocational training for boys incorporated the white man's agricultural way of life on a 75-acre school farm, different from their centuries-old hunting and gathering methods. Stressed in their curricula were how to raise a vegetable garden, milk a cow, harness a horse, build or mend a fence, and perform machine shop work. Girls learned sewing, cooking, washing, ironing, how to set a table and make a bed, and in some cases the rudiments of dairy work. All were drilled in discipline, regularity, cleanliness, neatness, and efficiency.

Before the first decade of the 1900s had ended, animosity toward the school developed from both Indian Valley whites and Native Americans. Parents from the latter group began resenting the "whitening" of their children. By 1900, the school commissioner wrote in his annual report that it was "nearly impossible to induce the nearby Indians to patronize the school." In 1918, eight Maidu were enrolled at the public school in Genesee Valley. The Greenville Indian School, attended by 100 out-of-county Native Americans, burned down again in 1921. Few were unhappy or overly concerned.

The Maidu continue to maintain their deep respect for Mother Earth, nature, conservation, and ecology. They are hospitable and gracious and enjoy their mountain way of life. There is a clear awakening of pride in their past and present. Cultural plurality is their present way of life. Cooperation with mainstream America is carried on by most, while at the same time, some seek to redefine and practice their old values and customs.

Young men like those in this c. 1895 photo wore uniforms at the Indian Mission School in Greenville where they learned English and vocational skills.

2. MINING: RICHES IN GOLD AND COPPER

The discovery of gold at Sutter's Fort in 1848 started the largest human migration in United States history. Locals became gold miners and, within a year, the first '49ers from the east coast arrived by boats in San Francisco. What was to become Plumas County was an unknown, unexplored country. No one knew anything about the area, but Peter Lassen, a transplanted Dane, had pioneered the Lassen Trail across northern Plumas in 1847.

Discovered in 1848 by Chico resident John Bidwell, Bidwell's Bar was a prosperous gold camp on the Middle Fork Feather River about 1.5 miles from its junction with the North Fork, approximately 9 miles from today's Oroville. With Native American labor, John Bidwell took out more than $100,000 in gold in 1848 and 1849. By 1853, Bidwell's Bar, with 2,000 people, was the most populous town in Butte County, as well as the county seat.

Between 1850 and 1855, the town developed Butte County's first newspaper, a school, two hotels, post office, combination courthouse and church, drugstore, clothing store, bookstore, bakery, restaurant, livery stable, steam sawmill, jail, and three express companies: Adams and Company, Everts, Snell and Company, and Feather River Express. A four-wire suspension bridge, 240 feet long and 15 feet wide, crossed the Middle Fork to the town. Lake Oroville, completed in 1969, now covers Bidwell's Bar.

During the late fall of 1849, gold rush immigrant Thomas Stoddard arrived at a mining camp on the Yuba River with his pockets full of gold. Tom was injured, exhausted, and weak from lack of food. He and his party used the Lassen Trail, an excessively long detour, beginning in west-central Nevada, then ranging northwest toward Goose Lake, Oregon until reaching the Pit River. They followed the Pit River's southwestern course toward Mt. Lassen and the Feather River region to Lassen's Rancho near present-day Red Bluff.

While in the Big Meadows area, Stoddard and a partner left their party to hunt for deer. After hours of hunting, they gave up. Meanwhile, their group had continued on and Stoddard was unable to relocate them. For several days, Stoddard and his companion wandered about, lost somewhere between Sierra Valley and Downieville. Coming upon a large lake, they saw what appeared

Rich Bar, on the Middle Fork Feather River, was the site of large flumes used to bare the bed of the river. Miners are shown toiling in the riverbed while cabins and shanties have been erected on the banks. This print was made from an 1851 oil painting that has since been lost.

to be gold nuggets gleaming from among the moss along the water's edge. After gathering as much gold as their pockets could carry, the two exhausted men fell asleep.

The next morning, Native Americans attacked them. Stoddard was injured and his companion was never heard from again. Stoddard worked his way through the mountains until at last he reached the North Fork of the Yuba River and the gold camps in the Downieville–Nevada City region. Stoddard told his tale to the miners, who immediately wanted to go back and find the lake.

The news traveled throughout the mining camps during the winter of 1849 and 1850; Gold Lake was the number one news item from Downieville to Monterey. Marysville merchant Peter Decker said in early December there was "much talk now of the Feather River Diggings." An unusual lack of rain implied lack of snow to some adventurous miners. One party intent on reaching the upper Middle Fork of the Feather River in December returned to the valley safely after running into deep snow that had begun the second half of November. Several members of another group died as a result of their attempt and another lost his toes due to frostbite. Following a month of mostly fine, clear, sunny weather, Peter Decker reported in February that miners were daily passing through Marysville toward the new town of Oroville and the Feather River country.

During the winter and spring of 1849 and 1850, substantial numbers of miners actively worked the Feather River around Bidwell's Bar and into the foothills nearby. In March and April, when snows began melting in the mountains, many moved further up the Middle Fork to Bingham's Bar near the present Butte–Plumas County line. When the 1849 and 1850 winter snows were gone, a multitude of anxious miners swarmed into the mountains to find Gold Lake in what would later become Plumas and Sierra Counties.

Abraham Taylor, age 30, and two friends were mining at Bingham's Bar on the Middle Fork where he learned from Maidu tribesmen of a rich mining bar only "three sleeps" away in the higher country. Anxious to begin prospecting, Taylor decided in mid-April 1850 to ascend the mountains with his two companions, Arnold and Fisher. The tale seemed worth looking into.

Supplied with provisions and optimism, the threesome moved up the divide between the Yuba and Feather Rivers to Little Grass Valley near today's La Porte. Turning north, they traveled to what became known as Stag Point on the south bank of the Middle Fork of the Feather River. The river water, however, was too deep, cold, and powerful to progress upstream in it. There were so many obstacles that 2 to 3 miles a day were all a man could accomplish traveling beside the river. After progressing upstream four tortuous days, prospecting intermittently and finding nothing, and with supplies running low, Arnold and Fisher had had enough, so the group decided to return to the valley.

Nevertheless, Taylor was still intrigued and, in late April or early May, with four new companions, he decided to try again. At Strawberry Valley, they met John Bodley with his two fully loaded wagons of provisions, liquor, and mining tools. Bodley knew that by summer the mountains would be full of miners looking for Gold Lake and rich diggings. Learning from Bodley of his intention to find a place to establish a trading post, Taylor led him to Little Grass Valley, where Bodley claimed the land and opened his store.

Having different plans, Taylor and his partners went to the Middle Fork again and repeated Taylor's previous trek. After a few days, they came upon an acre-sized gravel bar on the river and decided to make rockers. They promptly began averaging 2 to 4 ounces of gold per day. Within a month, more miners followed them. Before long, dozens arrived at Taylor's diggings. A canvas and brush mining camp sprang up like magic.

Tom Stoddard was on his way, too. In the mining camps, he exhibited nugget samples from his golden lake and a scar inflicted by the Native Americans. For his trip, he organized a select group of 25 men to accompany him. Supplies and mules were gathered and, about the last week of May, the expedition started for the Sierra, followed by nearly 500 to 1,000 other miners.

Stoddard led the excited mass toward the headwaters of the North Yuba River and Middle Fork of the Feather River. Finding the lake whose shores were lined with gold was foremost in their minds as they optimistically penetrated the mighty Sierra. All expected to discover Stoddard's Gold Lake beyond the next ridge. Days passed as the search continued. Gradually, uncertainty was born in the minds of

Ed Kelsey (center) looks over a prospect with a couple of miners on his Mill Creek claims near American Valley in the early 1900s. The men are cleaning up the bedrock after a day's washing of gravel.

some. Morale diminished as confusion seemed to replace Stoddard's certainty as to Gold Lake's exact location. Lakes were found, but none was the one with the gold-strewn shores.

Soon the party reached the Sierra Valley. Discontentment now turned to open rebellion. A meeting was held and Stoddard was informed that if he was unable to find Gold Lake the next day, "he would be strung up to the limb of a tree and left for the birds to roost upon." That night, he quietly fled in the darkness and made his way back to the safety of the lower-elevation mining camps. Last Chance Creek near Chilcoot and Humbug Valley near Portola both vie for namesake status as the location where Stoddard was given his ultimatum.

Without the benefit of Stoddard's guidance, others willing to believe the wondrous tale decided to search for his fabled lake. Steve and James Fowler recorded in their diary on June 15, 1850 that while in Plumas, near Marysville, some members of their company had departed with their mules for a "place called Gold Lake where it is said they take out one ounce to the panful."

During that same week, Bidwell's Bar miner Charles R. Parke wrote in his diary, "real excitement prevails along the river regarding the discovery at a certain 'Gold Lake' on the headwaters of the South Yuba River. Every pan of dirt is said to yield from $32 to $200. Six of our company have packed their mules and gone in search of the hidden treasure." Charles Parke and his friends followed them a few days later.

Excitement was peaking by mid-June. The June 17, 1850 *Marysville Placer Times* reported the Gold Lake frenzy as being the most amazing event of the year, where 10 ounces were said to be the "average yield to the panful." A party of 60 had already left Marysville heading for Gold Lake under the guidance of one prospector, who claimed to have already been there and returned extremely successful. He assured the group they would each harvest a minimum of $500 per day. Another guide led a party of 40 from Marysville toward Gold Lake on the condition each member pay him $100 upon their successful arrival and verification of his story, offering to forfeit his life for any untruth. A third leader departed with "a much larger party, who are to give him $200 each and the same forfeit of his life if there is any deception."

Two hundred others also departed in their Gold Lake quest with some 400 mules and provisions. Such was the magnitude of the excitement that at least 2,000 had left Marysville so far, the local newspaper reported. The price of mules and horses had doubled overnight and "were almost impossible to obtain." The June 19 *Sacramento Daily Transcript* reported, "places of business in Marysville are closed. The diggings at Gold Lake are probably the richest ever discovered."

From Peter Lassen's Ranch, J. Goldsborough Bruff wrote on June 20, 1850 of a "rumored discovery of immense deposits of gold, around a lake, situated somewhere between the upper waters of Feather and Yuva [Yuba] Rivers." During the following weeks, several companies left Lassen's Ranch to join the hunt and, on July 12, 1850, Peter Lassen himself became a part of the stampede to the higher mountains. Mountain man Jim Beckwourth closed the store he owned in Sonora to join the multitude hunting for Gold Lake. From Sacramento, George Baker wrote the following on June 23:

The Moseley brothers extracted gold and much loose dirt from a drift mine on the East Branch of North Fork Feather River c. 1890.

> A great excitement has pervaded this community for the last ten days in relation to "Gold Lake" where is reported to have been found the richest diggings of the country. All that is to be done there is "to sit down and pick it up!" I regard it all as a magnificent humbug. The lake is said to have an outlet into the North Fork of the Feather River. Some thousands have left for the place. The road is reported lined with the multitude.

Stoddard and the thousands of other hopeful prospectors never found Gold Lake.

After being threatened with lynching, Tom Stoddard left, but later returned to the Sierra, arriving at Downieville where he met Major William Downie, the founder of the town. Gold Lake dreams were obviously still in his heart, for by mid-October 1850, Stoddard, Downie, and a party of miners went to Poorman's Creek where they mined and wintered until the spring of 1851. During these blustery, snowy months, Stoddard alone harvested 200 pounds of gold. Downie considered him a man of "gentlemanly bearing and of more than ordinary education," but whose accounts were often ". . . incoherent. My impression is that he was not mentally balanced."

The Plumas County gold rush of 1850 was a direct result of the California Gold Rush and Stoddard's Gold Lake story. For the majority of miners who came to the Sierra in search of Gold Lake, disappointment dominated. For others, their perseverance paid off, resulting in discoveries at Nelson Creek, Poorman's Creek, Hopkins Creek, Onion Valley, Rich Bar, and Butte Bar. All provided rich diggings. Equally rewarding was a series of five mining bars on the East Branch of the North Fork of the Feather River: Rich Bar, Indian Bar, Smith Bar, French Bar, and Junction Bar.

Near the end of the third week of June, two members of a prospecting party, Nelson and Betterton, discovered gold on Nelson Creek, approximately 7 miles southeast of Quincy. Nelson Creek proved exceedingly rich as miners working in the creek obtained up to an ounce of gold dust, flakes, and nuggets per pan. Miners began flocking to the new diggings. Early-day miner James Larison went so far as to say, "Nelson Creek was good for $1,000 to the foot. Twenty feet on each side of the creek was all anyone could claim."

Seven weeks after discovery, many miners on or near Nelson Creek were daily gathering 18 to 25 ounces. Claims on the creek sold for $250 per foot. Before long, 1,000 miners had crowded in and Nelson Point grew in leaps and bounds. A saloon, a general store, and a boarding house-hotel shared the steep creek banks where Nelson Creek emptied into the Middle Fork of the Feather River.

A group known as the Wisconsin Company was among those seeking paydirt on Nelson Creek. During the summer, they "hit the jackpot." Calling their site Meeker Flat after one of their members, they took out 93 pounds of the precious metal in three weeks.

Less than 5 miles away was Poorman's Creek, where one man took out 125 ounces in half a day and 150 ounces the next. Edward McIlhaney, a mule pack train owner, stated that upon his arrival the creek was "filled from one end to the other with miners taking out thousands of dollars, the gold being mostly coarse." McIlhaney himself obtained a 78-ounce nugget plucked from the creek. An extremely fortunate miner from the state of Ohio found a 6.5-pound nugget in Poorman's Creek and another miner said the creek was so "dog-gone" rich that many large nuggets were sometimes unable to pass through the prongs of his sluice-fork. William Tell Parker tells of 100 men in late October grubbing out as much as 6 ounces daily.

Poorman's Creek flows into Hopkins Creek and at this junction was the town of Hopkinsville. About a mile or so upstream was another camp known as The Forks of Hopkins. Both camps were extremely rich and all the way down Hopkins Creek to its confluence with Nelson Creek, the stream was lined with miners.

Poorman's, Hopkins, and Nelson Creeks all feed into the Middle Fork of the Feather River, an impressive watercourse plunging powerfully down through a rocky, rugged canyon. For eons, the Middle Fork has been a carrier of auriferous gravels. These gold-rich gravels found homes in the sandbars, bedrock, crevices, and several dozen or more half-acre to acre size bars between Jamison Creek and Bidwell's Bar.

First to find a rich location on the north side of the river were Captain Blackburn and B.F. Chafee. The two staked their claims and returned to Stringtown on the South Fork of the Feather River above Bidwell's Bar for supplies. Upon their

In this 1902 photo, the Nelson Gold Mine is shown perched on the steep mountainside near Nelson Point. These men drove a long tunnel into the hill to retrieve the gold. The earth was brought out in the car shown and dumped at the end of the track to be washed later.

Gold was released from ancient river channels by water forced through nozzles at North American Hydraulic Mine near La Porte, c. 1900.

return, they were startled to find their location swarming with a multitude of others, rockers and cradles being as plentiful as boulders. Foremost among this new group were William T. Ballou and Bill Poole, the latter finding "a nugget as big as a hen's egg." This new horde had, however, honored Blackburn's and Chafee's claims at what they called Rich Bar (not to be confused with Rich Bar on the North Feather), and likewise took up generous-sized claims.

Their campfires and tents "presented the appearance of a vast army" and attracted an additional multitude of newcomers until those without claims far exceeded those fortunate enough to have one. Demanding a "miners' meeting," the majority without claims won their appeal, forcing a reduction of claim sizes to 40 feet by 40 feet.

One company built a two-sided wing dam in the river itself, which yielded rich deposits. Most deserted Rich Bar as winter neared, but many more came back the next spring. Rich Bar was only one of dozens of gold strikes on the Middle Fork. Fell's Bar, Poplar Bar, Bell's Bar, Peoria Bar, Bray's Bar, Hottentot Bar, Sailor Bar, Columbia Bar, Minerva Bar, Butte Bar, and many others all produced rich returns. Bar and bank mining boomed and many wing dams were put in. To build these dams and work the riverbed, flumes had to be constructed from sawn lumber. At the foot of Rich Bar, J.B. Batchelder's sawmill, the first in Plumas County, supplied the boards.

Around the turn of the century, the Pioneer Hotel at Onion Valley was a typical stage stop along the Quincy–La Porte Road. The proprietress was said to be "drunk all the time," so the teamsters ate at the nearby Mullen Hotel.

Pilot Peak tops the main ridge used for a trail between Marysville and the Feather River diggings. Lying at the northwestern base of Pilot Peak is 6,300-foot Onion Valley. Using Pilot Peak as a beacon, Onion Valley became the hub for the rich mining camps on Poorman's, Hopkins, and Nelson Creeks, and the Middle Fork. In July 1850, a party of 130 prospectors reached Onion Valley. While stopping for water and a rest, they noted the wild onions growing in profusion in the valley and on the mountain slopes, which resulted in naming the location Onion Valley.

A member of this party known as "One-Eyed Moore" found about 200 ounces, while another unearthed 375 ounces in an hour and a half, including a 112-ounce nugget and several smaller ones of 30 ounces. A few days later, a large quartz boulder was turned over and, from the soil beneath it, half a hat-full of gold was picked up.

Onion Valley grew rapidly and, by 1851, had a population of 2,000 miners and merchants. Edward McIlhaney and Charles Thomas opened a combination hotel and general mercantile store, the only two-story building in town, and during the same year they began the area's first wheeled stage, running twice a week from Marysville to Onion Valley. Onion Valley's main street soon extended north and south across the valley, with a score of one-story wooden buildings. According to one source, a view of the town was as follows: "saloon, gambling house, store, saloon, restaurant, gambling hall, saloon, store, eating house, saloon, etc."

During the last week of June or first week of July 1850, a party of prospectors discovered a second Rich Bar when they reached the East Branch of the North Fork of the Feather River. Time has clouded history, but most evidence places the discovery event close to July 1, 1850. A rough composite of the event credits a German named Spreckles with making the initial discovery. Early in the morning when going to the river for water to make coffee, he spotted a 2-ounce nugget lying on the ground as he was passing over the head of the bar. He returned with a gold pan and promptly gathered 125 ounces of nuggets worth $2,000 from two pans of dirt. Staking out three claims of 40 feet each, over the next four days Spreckles and his two friends took out 2,250 ounces, or $36,000 at $16 per ounce.

Rich Bar became the most famous placer mining gold camp in Plumas County's history, and Louise Amelia Knapp Smith Clappe became its most famous resident. "Dame Shirley," as Clappe was to become known, became a prominent California gold rush celebrity with the publication of *The Shirley Letters From the California Mines*. It is a compilation of the 23 letters she wrote to her sister back east during her stay near Rich Bar. Dame Shirley and her husband lived at Indian Bar in 1851 and 1852, and her letters, according to historian Josiah Royce, were "the best account of an early mining camp" that he ever knew.

This miner processes his golden gravel in a "rocker" or "cradle." Water was poured over the gravel in the "grizzly" while he rocked the machine back and forth. The agitation caused the heavier gold to fall through the holes and lodge behind riffles, while the lighter dirt washed away.

Dame Shirley's letters are considered a minute, detailed description of Rich Bar's existence—a perfect mirror of the society in which she lived. As she told her sister, "I take great pains to describe things exactly as I see them, hoping that thus you will obtain an idea of life in the mines as it is."

As much as $14 million to $23 million worth of gold was found at Rich Bar from July 1, 1850, to the turn of the twentieth century. About $2 million to $4 million in gold was found in 1850 and 1851. Downstream from Rich Bar there were seven more mining bars along a 2-mile stretch of the East Branch of the North Fork: Peasoup, Indian, Stony, Missouri, Smith, French, and Junction Bars. Locally and historically, these seven mining bars are referred to as the Rich Bar complex of mines.

Rich Bar alone was about a half-square mile in size. A population of 2,500 lived, mined, and worked at Rich Bar in 1852. It was the most populous of the seven mining camps and was the principal business location where three or four general stores existed, along with a butcher shop, bakery, several tent saloons—one with a billiard table—some gambling tents, and one blacksmith shop. The Empire Hotel in "downtown Rich Bar" was the busiest and most prominent structure, being a combination hotel, general store, restaurant, bar, and gambling room. Milk was delivered once or twice a week from a secluded ranch 5 miles away by a steep and rugged trail. A one-lane bowling hall was in Indian Bar.

Smith Bar, located 1 mile downstream from Rich Bar, produced even richer returns than Rich Bar in 1850. Indian Bar competed favorably with the other six bars on the East Branch for the most number of gold nuggets found in 1851. Rich Bar was a typical California gold camp. Murders, vigilante committees, hangings, and a $20,000 poker pot at a gambling hall were among the impassioned events occurring there.

Gold is found in odd places. At Rich Bar on the East Branch, Dame Shirley said gold was so abundant that even an "ignorant adventurer, who digs just for the sake of digging is almost sure to be successful." It was found from bedrock crevices in the Feather River's bottom to the top of 7,447-foot Eureka Peak, near Johnsville.

By 1851, most of the mining camps and streams were mobbed to overflowing. In late May 1851, a party of nine of the overflow group decided to move toward the east-central part of the county. They stopped to camp at the base of a large mountain and two of the group, Merethew and Peck, decided to climb it. They spotted a decomposed quartz vein about 20 feet wide protruding several feet above the surface for nearly 400 feet about 200 feet from the top of the mountain. All along the decomposed vein, loose nuggets were found while others were clearly visible on the edge, but still imbedded in the rock.

Using their penknives, the men began prying the nuggets out. Merethew and Peck descended to invite the other seven members back to the top of what they began calling Gold Mountain. The party began using hammers and picks to remove the nuggets from the rock. They soon began the expensive investment in equipment essential to obtain the lode's gold. By June 5, 1851, they had organized an outfit of 36 men to share expenses and named their group the Eureka Company.

Miners and carpenters pose at the entrance to the famous Plumas Eureka Mine in Johnsville. Note that these men in 1905 are wearing soft hats, prior to the advent of hardhats and carbide lamps.

Since establishment of ownership rights for hard rock claims was not yet clear, the Eureka Company used placer ownership principles and each took out a mining claim of 30 square-feet. Thinking ahead, they also took possession of a nearby lake to provide water for power.

While the Eureka Company concluded these preliminaries, other miners who learned of their discovery soon began arriving. The second group that came to Eureka Peak consisted of 76 men who located their mine well up the mountainside, 1,500 feet above Jamison Creek. They took out water privileges and laid out a town adjacent to Jamison Creek, which they named "City of Seventy-six." A 16-stamp mill was erected at the City of Seventy-six and a chute-way was made to move the quartz from the mine to the stamp mill. Unfortunately, when the mill started in 1852, 42 tons of ore yielded only $200 "and with a huge disgust most of the company scattered to the four winds." During the ensuing months two other companies of miners, The Mammoth and The Rough and Ready, also began efforts to mine on Eureka Peak.

Nearby Mexican miners were familiar with hard rock gold extraction processes and showed the Eureka Company members how to make primitive arrastras. These devices consisted of a foot-high rock wall in a 10- to 15-foot diameter circle. Gold-bearing rocks up to 10 inches in diameter from the quartz vein were dropped into the arrastra. Mercury, or quicksilver, was added to the arrastra and a mule, harnessed to a wooden cross-arm on one end and a large rock on the other

31

end, walked in a circle around a center post serving as a pivot. The mule walked in a circle all day, dragging the rock as it gradually broke up the smaller rocks, exposing the gold, which was then collected.

The Chile Wheel, developed in South America, was another extraction method soon introduced. The wheel consisted of a circular enclosure similar to the arrastra, but instead of drag stones being used to grind the quartz into powder, a large stone wheel attached to the horizontal shaft was used for grinding the rock. The freed gold was saved with mercury in the same manner as the arrastra.

Many in the Eureka Company became discouraged with this slow process until finally most of the 36 miners decided to leave for new diggings. They leased their portions of Eureka Peak to a company of Mexicans, who agreed to pay them 25 percent of the gold they successfully extracted. The Mexicans worked with the arrastras on and off until 1861, some of the rock paying $60 to $100 per ton.

Other Eureka Company members plugged away, borrowed San Francisco money, and in 1855, erected a 12-stamp mill to crush the gold-bearing quartz. Each of the 12 stamps in the mill were on the bottom end of a solid iron rod 8 inches in diameter and weighing 800 pounds, standing next to each other in a battery. A water-powered overshot wheel raised the stamps 8.5 inches and then gravity brought them down with a tremendous force. The hard quartz was pulverized by 80 crushing strokes per minute. Each stamp crushed 2.5 tons of ore per day.

The Mammoth Company located along the northeast side of the mountain adjoining the Eureka. Similar to the Seventy-six Company operations, they dug their tunnel, extracted ore, and used arrastras and Chile wheels. The results were good and they set up a 12-stamp mill next to Jamison Creek. They constructed a 3,000-foot-long railway from the mine to carry ore to the mill. By 1868, the Mammoth had yielded $400,000.

The Rough and Ready Company established their claims on the southeastern side of the mountain about a half-mile from the Seventy-six Company holdings. They dug a chute from the mine to their 12-stamp mill also beside Jamison Creek. A railway replaced the chute in 1852. Operations were suspended in 1854, later resumed, and then stopped permanently in 1857.

Discoveries continued during the summer of 1852 when gold was found at what became known as Elizabethtown, 2 miles north of Quincy. In the spring of 1852, Alexander and Frank Tate discovered gold at Tate's Ravine just north of Quincy. That fall, Lewis Stark and a number of others traveling the Beckwourth Trail stopped nearby to prospect. After several days, they had panned out 1 ounce of gold. They began using a rocker and a few days later found a 28-ounce nugget and then a 50-ounce nugget. A small camp was set up, and by 1853, 3,000 inhabitants were settled around Elizabethtown. Within a few years, stores, saloons, boarding houses, gambling establishments, hotels, a fireproof store, several two-story buildings, and a dance hall made up the town. By 1854, a Sons of Temperance Lodge, Masonic Lodge, post office, and the county's first school (without a building) were added. Lewis Stark was the first postmaster and since his daughter Elizabeth was the only single young lady in town, the chivalrous miners bestowed her name upon the town. Elizabethtown was the county's most thriving settlement during the mid-1850s. Today, all that remains is a historical monument erected in 1927 and the foundation ruins of Blood & Shannon's fireproof store, uncovered by floods in 1997.

Further south, Gold Lakers found color in Little Grass Valley in the fall of 1850. A few miles away the next year, similar finds were made at Rabbit Creek. Activity increased along Rabbit Creek in 1852 and the first two cabins were built there that year. The next year saw the use of the labor saving method of ground sluicing introduced in 1851 at various Mother Lode locations. To ground sluice, a ditch was dug from a creek at a point higher up and directed down the hillside, carrying the eroded paydirt to a waiting sluice box. Thus, the moving water carrying the paydirt through the sluice box did a substantial amount of work for the miner. Miners soon found that they could place a hose in the water ditch and direct it to their claim by "piping" the water a short distance to the desired spot. Ditches were dug from upper Rabbit Creek to provide gravity flow and piping activity prospered.

In time, an ancient river channel running through the Rabbit Creek diggings was discovered. Although much gold was recovered initially, the channel soon disappeared into the hillside. To get back down to the ancient channel's bedrock, a more sophisticated method of mining than ground sluicing was required.

The Quincy band played at the "plaza" in Elizabethtown in this c. 1858 image, the only known photograph of that early Plumas County town, which was established because of rich gold discoveries.

Hydraulic mining was the answer. Edward Matteson is credited with the invention in 1853 at Nevada City. He simply put a nozzle on the hose where he was piping and by reducing the outlet, he increased the water pressure. Hydraulic mining was born. The idea spread, and by 1854 hydraulic mining was being used at Rabbit Creek to make huge cuts in the mountain's side. Over the next few years, Rabbit Creek (the name of which was changed to La Porte in 1857) reported a number of homes, a butcher shop, blacksmith shop, tin shop, sawmill, express office, Wells Fargo and Company office, several banks, a newspaper, bowling alley, hotel, general mercantile store, brewery, and post office.

La Porte reached its zenith in 1862, boasting three hotels, six large stores, 14 saloons (two-thirds of which had adjoining dance halls), a stable, a tenpin bowling alley, an opera house, Chinese laundry, Methodist-Episcopalian and Catholic churches, two meeting halls, and scores of miners' cabins and residences. Within a radius of 10 miles, $93 million in gold was extracted. One of the nuggets weighed slightly more than 417 pounds, the largest gold nugget ever found in the United States. In 1866, the county line between Sierra and Plumas was adjusted to annex La Porte to Plumas County. Distance and dissatisfaction with the county seat in Downieville was one of the reasons for the adjustment. Hydraulic mining activity in the La Porte area flourished for four decades, from the early 1850s to about 1890, when the 1884 Anti-Debris Act passed by the state legislature to curtail dumping debris into the rivers finally took effect.

The Native Sons of the Golden West, an organization comprised of history-minded California natives, played an active role in La Porte's social development. In this 1900 photo they parade down Main Street in downtown La Porte.

David Kirkham was one of the first to find gold at North Fork (Seneca) on the North Fork of the Feather River in 1852. Numerous placer and quartz discoveries were made there and in the surrounding hills over the next 50 years. Mining has continued on and off there to the present day.

In the Meadow Valley-Mountain House region west of Quincy laid a large belt of gold-bearing gravels. The problem was how to get water to them. Companies of three or more men organized for the purpose of digging ditches to their mining claims. Each ditch was 1 to 3 feet deep and wide, carrying water from a stream or lake higher up in the mountains to their mining grounds. In 1855, the Plumas Ditch was dug 7 miles from Gold Lake to Silver Lake to the Mountain House area. The Plumas Water Company constructed this ditch for its water-powered sawmill and for sale of water to the miners at Mountain House and Fales Hill. Upon completion of the Plumas Ditch, the mining town of Mt. Pleasant sprang up with a population of 500 people. Lost to time and later mining, no dwellings and only scant traces survive.

The Spanish Ranch Ditch, 18 miles in length, was dug from below Mountain House on Spanish Creek west to Elizabethtown. Branch lines were run to Gopher Hill, Badger Hill, Railroad Hill, and Shores Hill, all along Spanish Creek.

Placer deposits were found in early 1860 on the north slope of the mountain below Round Valley, a couple of miles from what became Greenville. John Ellis bought out discoverers Palmer and Newlands and began prospecting and mining the quartz ledges. Returns were good enough to warrant construction of a 24-stamp mill.

As additional discoveries were made, Round Valley quickly became a bustling gold camp and "one of the most important" of the Feather River diggings of the early 1860s. By 1862, the town of Round Valley had a population of 378, of whom 300 were men, 28 women, and 50 children. The town had three general stores, four saloons, a hotel, livery stable, gambling halls, a sawmill, school, and several other buildings. Wells, Fargo and Company set up an express office in town and Fenton Whiting made weekly mail trips with his Feather River Express.

In 1861, J.B. Batchelder located a rich lode above Crescent Mills that soon became Henry C. Bidwell's Green Mountain Mine. Nearby, in 1862, discoveries were made at what became Cherokee on the northeast side of Round Valley. The camp soon boasted a general store, saloon, and hotel. To supply goods to the new mines, the town of Greenville was born in 1861 or 1862.

Between 1860 and 1880, 15 mines were operating in the Greenville area with a combined total of 314 stamps. The Green Mountain Mine alone had a daily payroll of 75 men. Greenville prospered due to the gold rush excitement. Within a decade of their discoveries, Round Valley and Cherokee were ghost towns. The Green Mountain, Crescent, and Droege each continued to be worked, on and off, until the early 1900s. The Green Mountain Mine produced $4 million during its operating years, twice that of the others. Gold was Greenville's cornerstone, but as the precious mineral played out, agriculture and ranching became its next 100-year destiny.

In the south-central part of the county was Sawpit Flat. Located a mile or so west of Onion Valley, it was an extremely rich drift mining area. A half mile west of it was the hydraulic mining locale of Richmond Hill. Drift mining was Sawpit Flat's necessary method of mining. A company of miners would dig a tunnel up to 5,000 feet or more into the mountain's side until they reached the ancient riverbed. At this point, a new tunnel called a "drift" turned to follow the paydirt located along the bedrock of the ancient stream. All winter, drift mining was performed, the paydirt being deposited outside the tunnel's entrance waiting for spring and water.

The *Plumas National* newspaper reported in June 1867 that "the Eagle Company cleaned up last week the sum of $28,000" or 1,250 ounces. Returns for the New York Company amounted to 1,200 ounces. Two years later, the same company's spring cleanup amounted to 1,515 ounces of gold dust. Another account tells of 130 to 200 ounces being "washed up every 36 hours." By the end of June, the newspaper reported, "The miners of Sawpit Flat have about finished cleaning up their season's work. The claims have paid unusually well. Sawpit is one of the best mining camps in the state."

By 1870, San Francisco banker John Parrott and his financial company had by various means obtained ownership of the Eureka, Washington, and Rough and Ready Companies—all except the Mammoth. Parrott understood money and proper business practices well, so he hired a professional hard rock mining superintendent and a workforce of 100 men. By April 1871, the Eureka began yielding $1,000 a day and by summer's end, $100,000 had been mined. With these figures, John Parrott decided he might sell his combined holdings.

Parrott approached a group of British investors who owned the Sierra Buttes Mine, 15 miles away. Impressed by his holdings, the British investors purchased Parrott's holdings in 1872 and became known as the Plumas-Eureka Company. The new company's efficiency resulted in immediately profitable returns. Dividends of 15 percent per year were common throughout the 1870s. Over 26 years (1871 to 1897), the Plumas-Eureka Mine had a gross output of $17 million.

Eureka Mills, high on the mountain at the entrance to the company's tunnel, rapidly grew into a year-round mining town. By 1873, it had a boarding house for 200 single miners, a new stamp mill, a hotel, two stores, a school, a church, a boot making store, three saloons, a blacksmith shop, and numerous family dwellings. Because of the steep hillside, some structures had foundation posts 16 feet long on one side to create a level floor.

Near present-day Johnsville, a sawmill was built that immediately began cutting 25,000 board feet per day. A stamp mill was constructed, equipment sheds were erected, and by January 1873, a boarding house accommodating 200 men was completed. By July 1873, $150,000 had been spent in improvements; $300,000 by the end of 1874. A second boarding house built in 1873 is the present-day Plumas-Eureka State Park Museum.

Tunnel miners and blacksmiths worked 12 hours a day in the mid-1870s. Blasting-men used a 4-pound hammer and 16-inch drill made by the blacksmiths to drive holes into the face of the tunnel. The holes were packed with black powder and fuses and, when detonated, blasted loose chunks of rock. The rocks were loaded into ore cars using shovels and wheelbarrows and a mule on iron tracks pulled each full ore car to the tunnel entrance.

In 1875, William Johns became superintendent of the Plumas-Eureka Mine and overall operations became even more efficient and prosperous. The Plumas-Eureka complex of tunnels extends over 62 miles, with the longest tunnel at 1,500 feet. Under Johns's leadership, there was a marked increase in tunnel construction, and improvements in living conditions for the workers and their families. A brand new 40-stamp mill called the Mohawk Mill was completed in 1878 about 150 yards from today's museum.

An aerial tramway was built to move the quartz ore down the mountainside to the Mohawk Mill. The ore, transported to the tunnel entrance, was loaded into large buckets hanging on a 1,700-foot cable and lowered to the mill. Besides moving ore, some say the tramway also hauled skiers, becoming the world's first ski lift!

The Mohawk Mill was constructed inside a large wooden building for year-round operation. It was powered by water in summer and steam in winter. Today, the restored Mohawk stamp mill is one of the highlights for visitors to the Plumas-Eureka State Park. The stamp mill processed 40,000 to 50,000 tons of ore per year. This activity required breaking up and processing 2.5 tons of rock to obtain 1 ounce of gold. The quartz ore was removed from the large buckets at the Mohawk Mill and dumped into mechanical crushers, which reduced the quartz rocks into marble-sized pieces. The stamp mill further pulverized the ore into

In sleepy Johnsville during the 1920s, just waiting for the mail could turn into a social event. This scene is quite different from 30 or 40 years earlier when the town was a bustle of activity due to the Plumas Eureka Mine and the Jamison Mine.

beach sand consistency, which was then subjected to the "chlorination process." During the 1850s and 1860s, almost 50 percent of the gold was lost using the arrastra and Chile wheel, but by the late 1860s and early 1870s, the loss ratio was less than 10 percent due to the chlorination process. The gold was made into bullion bars and shipped to a British bank in San Francisco.

Although the flat land along the Johnsville ledge near the Mohawk Mill operations seemed a favorable choice for a town, not a single home or store was located there as 1875 began. John Banks changed that when he built the first house there that year. The next year, he enlarged it into a hotel and also erected a store. August Crazer built a brewery, and by 1879 Johnsville had two hotels, two stores, several stables, and more houses, and was now said to resemble "a town more than a village." Welsh, Scots, Germans, Italians, Greeks, and Serbs made up the mining town's population.

Inevitably, gambling dens, dance halls, saloons, and murders introduced their undesirable presence. In 1882, a fire almost completely destroyed the entire town; however, within a year, Johnsville had rebuilt. It now had two hotels, three general stores, two meat markets, several blacksmith shops, saloons, and an Odd Fellows Hall with 25 members. The first Johnsville post office opened in 1883.

To Plumas County, the Plumas-Eureka Mine was an important employer and tax base, being the county's largest employer. Over 325 men were working

Racing on longboard skis was highly competitive; the wax, or "dope," being a jealously guarded secret. These homemade skis were often as long as 14 feet and reached speeds of 88 mph!

in 1872, 400 in 1878, and nearly 250 were still at work in 1894. A post office at Eureka Mills was established in 1875 and the telegraph office was given the name Plumas-Eureka Mine. In 1873, the Plumas-Eureka Mine was assessed by the county at $930,000, resulting in tax revenues of approximately $15,000. Since all the rest of Plumas County did not total a combined assessment of more than $300,000, it is very clear the British were contributing a great share of tax money to Plumas County. Though worked out and finally sold in 1903, the Plumas-Eureka Mine was clearly one of Plumas County's quartz bonanzas.

In 1871, the Plumas Mining & Water Company was organized with a capital stock of $150,000 and purchased the Plumas Ditch, Spanish Ranch Ditch, and a number of smaller ones. These ditches enabled their mines at Gopher Hill and Badger Hill to provide enormous returns. In 1874, 4.5-inch and 7-inch hydraulic monitors were placed in the pit of Gopher Hill and began assaulting the tertiary placers. Proceeds of $500 (30 ounces) a day; $1,885 (104 ounces) the first eight days in May; and $28,000 (1,750 ounces) "in a few weeks" were examples of yields recorded in the 1870s. Plumas Mining & Water Company continued productive operations until the state finally forced closure of hydraulic mining activity in 1889, a result of the passage of the Sawyer Decision of 1884. This anti-debris ruling effectively shut down hydraulic mining activity. During its lifetime, Gopher Hill alone had yielded $21 million. Its rugged scars are easily recognized along Spanish Creek between Quincy and Meadow Valley.

Located less than 3 miles from the county courthouse in downtown Quincy, Hungarian Hill was known to have "yielded prodigiously" in earlier rocker and long-tom days; new owners with capital obtained the hilltop claims in the early 1870s. "A large force of Chinamen" was hired to dig a 7-mile ditch from Mill Creek to Hungarian Hill and a shorter ditch of 1 mile from Slate Creek. Thousands of feet of huge iron pipe and 1,800 feet of wooden flumes were used when needed to cross creeks, ravines, gulches, and solid rock segments. The pipes were 15 to 22 inches in diameter, while wooden flumes were 32 inches deep and varied in width from 4 to 8 feet. Branch ditches led to four large reservoirs within the Hungarian Hill diggings where natural terrain provided three walls.

Four hydraulic monitors, the largest having an "eight inch nozzle manifesting prodigious force," threw a jet of some 1,000 inches of water under 300 feet of pressure against the hillside. The bank seemed to fairly "melt" before the almost irresistible power where basketball-sized rocks weighing up to 200 pounds were tossed about like pebbles. The water and paydirt matrix were directed into a sluice box and two undercurrents making it almost impossible for any gold to escape.

Jet streams attacked the mountainsides 24 hours a day for months at a time. One week yielded 108 ounces; $1,400 (87 ounces) in nine days; and $50,000 (3,125 ounces) was taken out by the first week of April 1873. In 1876, $41,000 (2,562 ounces) was the pay for eight months work. Hungarian Hill placers paid well.

The Dutch Hill diggings are located along the very top of a mountain ridge at an elevation of 4,800 feet about 6 miles southwest of Big Meadows (Lake

Long after Plumas Eureka Mine's closure, a mine car was still poised as if ready to roll to dump chutes, through which ore was sent to be crushed, releasing gold from quartz rock.

Almanor) and 1 mile north of present-day Seneca and the North Fork of the Feather River. Dutch Hill opened as a major hydraulic mine in the 1870s, although placer mining and drift mining had worked very well there in the 1860s. At that time, some companies of miners had made as much as $1,000 a day. In 1873, Sacramento capitalists purchased the Dutch Hill mining claims and incorporated under the name of North Fork Mining Company with a capital stock of $500,000.

Surveyors traveled all the way to Rice Creek in present-day Lassen Volcanic National Park, 33 miles from Dutch Hill, before they were satisfied they could obtain a seven-month supply of water. Engineers, blasters, and laborers were hired, and the mammoth project of constructing the Dutch Hill Ditch was undertaken in 1874. Rice Creek waters were diverted upon leaving present-day Lassen Park through a tunnel 1,150 feet long, 6.5 feet high, and 5 feet wide. After leaving the tunnel in Tehama County, the Rice Creek waters ran a short distance into Tule Lake, now called Wilson Lake. From that point, the water moved through a cut in solid lava 660 feet long, 7 feet wide, and 11 feet at the deepest point. From this cut, the water was conveyed in a 924-foot-long wooden flume placed on a solid lava foundation, concluding at the edge of the timber where segments of the water ditch were more easily dug by hand.

Normal ditch digging was done for just 20 percent of the next 15 miles, since granite covered the other 80 percent. This required blasting, making ditch line construction more difficult. Still the ditch continued to wind its way ever so slowly to Deer Creek Pass on the ridge between Butte and Deer Creeks, into Plumas County where it continued to twist and turn several miles more until it reached the side of Stover Mountain overlooking Big Meadows. From there, 8 miles of pipe was laid toward the upper end of Butt Valley.

Sheets of iron for the 8 miles of pipe were ordered from Pittsburgh, Pennsylvania and shipped to Chico. Ten-mule teams pulled wagons burdened with 12,000 pounds per load up the heavy grade from Chico to a convenient location known as Pipetown. At this site, just west of present-day Prattville, blacksmiths fashioned the sheets into pipes.

From the east end of the pipe near Butt Valley, a 6-foot-wide by 3-foot-deep ditch carried the water 6 miles to the ridge dividing Clear Creek from Butt Valley. At this point, a second tunnel 835 feet long was dug. From here, the waters continued their journey to the existing Ohio Creek Ditch and on to Dutch Hill. By early 1875, the $200,000 ditch from present-day Lassen Volcanic National Park to Dutch Hill was finished. In all, there were 33 miles of ditch, pipe, and flume.

A 50-man crew aimed hydraulic monitors at the gravel faces while others increased their drift mining efforts because of the new supply of water. From the very beginning of spring 1875, Dutch Hill operations were paying "six ounces per day to the man." A cleanup of 23 days of hydraulic operations recovered 600 ounces and $30,000 to $40,000 (1,900 to 2,500 ounces) in another four-week stint.

Placer miners had been working Wolf Creek near Greenville since the 1850s with ever-diminishing returns until, by the 1870s, those still working the creek were barely making wages. A new quartz discovery changed the situation in 1875. Henry C. Bidwell and Charles H. Lawrence learned of the new discovery and purchased it for $8,000 in 1876. Called the Gold Stripe Mine, a 24-stamp mill was erected there and George Standart was hired as superintendent. He soon had 35 to 40 tons of ore being crushed every 24 hours. During the first three weeks of January 1877, the Gold Stripe yielded $6,400 (400 ounces). The nearby Wisconsin Mine with its ten-stamp mill was paying $9 per ton.

In February 1877, the *Plumas National Bulletin* reported the Wolf Creek quartz mines "are developing magnificently. Capital has found its way there, and the shipments from the Gold Stripe and other mines prove that the investment is a good one."

In 1880, gold-bearing quartz discoveries were made at Rush Creek and Rich Gulch. The richest was the quartz discovery at Rich Gulch located where Rush Creek joins the East Branch. The Elizabeth Consolidated Gold Mine extracted gold valued at $9 million there. During its peak years, the Elizabeth employed 135 men. A small mining town developed at the Rush Creek–East Branch junction.

Two major jolts occurred to curtail the mining industry: passage of the 1884 Sawyer Decision, or Anti-Debris Act, by the California state legislature, which ended disposal of hydraulic mining debris in the Sacramento and San Joaquin rivers; and the fall of gold productivity that deepened by the mid-1880s. Placer returns had steadily declined year by year since the 1850s. By the 1870s and 1880s, most of the placer grounds were abandoned to the Chinese. Wolf Creek quartz operations, the hydraulic mines of Meadow Valley and La Porte, and the continuing productivity of the Plumas Eureka Mine, all heavily capitalized, remained positive operations during this time.

Another of Plumas County's prosperous operations was developed by San Francisco capitalists in 1887. The site of their proposed quartz operation adjoined the Plumas-Eureka Mine on Little Jamison Creek. In 1890, a boarding house, superintendent's home, office and supply room, and a stable were built. Mine tunnel construction also began immediately. By the end of 1892, 1,700 feet of tunnel was finished. A new, large building housed an air compressor, water wheel, hoisting works, and an assay office to test the ores immediately. By 1894, an 1,800-foot drain tunnel was completed and, two years later, a ten-stamp mill was in operation, crushing 30 tons of ore per day. By 1897, the company was able to begin paying dividends.

A fire caused trouble in 1899, but repairs were made rapidly and in 1900, 60 tons of ore was being crushed daily by the 60-man work force. Electric lights were

The company town of Walkermine was built to support the work crews and their families. Thriving from 1920 until 1941, it held a store, bar, hospital, four bunkhouses, library, post office, theater, school, baseball field, ski hill, and other amenities. During winter it was cut off from the outside except by the 9-mile aerial tramway.

installed in the mine and all the buildings. From 1905 to 1908, the Jamison Mine was called the "leading producer of gold in Plumas County, the only important quartz mine now productive in the county." By 1908, the mine had 6,473 feet of drift tunnels and a crosscut tunnel of 1,500 feet.

The golden times were gone, however, and the Jamison Mine Company paid no dividends-in 1915. By 1919, officials decided all the valuable ore was exhausted and they sold the mine in 1921. Total production up to that time had been $2 million.

From World War I through the 1920s, small- to medium-size gold operations continued on a sporadic basis. A renewed burst of enthusiasm developed following President Franklin Roosevelt's 1934 increase in gold from $20.67 per ounce to $35. A dozen or two old quartz and hydraulic mines were re-opened and put into production right away, but within a few years, the mines were closed by the federal government during World War II.

Gold made a comeback at Virgilia during the 1930s when local owner Harley Flournoy began mining operations, but after digging a 40-foot shaft, he sold out to a group of San Francisco lawyers. Work by the new owners' 135-man crew produced 500-foot shafts and 1,700-foot tunnels. A 240-ton flotation mill was brought in to process the ore that averaged $13 to $14 a ton.

In September 1936, the *Indian Valley Record* stated an estimated $100,000 a year was still being taken from small mines. A State Division of Mines publication reported Plumas County gold production from 1880 (the first year it began keeping records) to 1934 had been $21,426,000.

Gold mining is now carried on as a recreational pursuit, but gold was Plumas County's cornerstone. Many of its old-time residents—and even newcomers—are proud of its golden heritage. Is there gold still out there? Remember, geologists tell us there's still twice as much remaining as was ever taken out!

During the 1920s and 1930s, Plumas County was number one in state copper production. Engels Mine on Lights Creek in northern Indian Valley produced $25 million over its lifetime, and Walker Mine, 15 miles south, put out $23 million. Jack and James Ford discovered copper outcroppings above the North Arm of Indian Valley during the Civil War, while others found similar deposits along Genesee's Ward Creek. The Chapman brothers at their primitive smelter in Genesee Valley further processed the rich, naturally concentrated metal.

It was not until the twentieth century that the Engels brothers secured financing to put the Engels and Superior ledges into production. Realizing that more money was needed to properly operate the copper mine, the Engels incorporated in 1901. Upper Camp, at the headwaters of China Gulch, so named for the placer stream once worked in the early years by the Chinese, was the site of the first Engels Mine mill to crush ore. It was also the site of the nation's first all-flotation mill for copper processing, installed in 1914. After a short time, it was decided to move the primary mill operations down to the older Lower Camp, along Lights Creek.

Copper concentrates were loaded on wagons and hauled by 12-horse teams over dirt roads to Keddie and the Western Pacific Railroad (WPRR) for $9 per ton. At Paxton, the contents were loaded on the WPRR trains and shipped to the American Smelting and Refining Company in Garfield, Utah. Bulldog Mack trucks were used for a short period in winter, but by 1917, both methods were replaced by the Indian Valley Railroad (IVRR). This line was built jointly by Engels Mine (85 percent) and the WPRR (15 percent). The tracks ran from Lower Camp to Paxton, named for Elmer E. Paxton, a prominent mine stockholder.

Six hundred men worked around the clock. Counting wives, children, and other residents, during the peak production years, 2,000 or more people resided at Lower Camp. Among the earliest structures at Lower Camp were the company mill, mine office, machine shop, general store, and dormitories for single male employees, boarding houses, and private homes. Next came the railroad depot, storerooms, amusement hall, hotel, post office, hospital, church, and school. The company hired a full-time physician, motion pictures were shown at the amusement hall, and the men formed a baseball team. The Sierra Syncopators and the Frisco Five were both dance bands that originated out of Engels Mine.

For nearly two decades, Engels Mine was not only one of the county's most successful business ventures, it was also the largest copper producing mine in the state. During more than 15 years of operations, Engels yielded 117 million pounds of copper, along with substantial amounts in gold and silver amounting to $2.56 million. Dividends were paid as early as 1916 and an assessment was never levied. When the price of copper dropped below operating costs in 1930, Engels Mine closed for good. Nothing remains but a large cement foundation on the hillside.

Walker Mine competed with Engels Mine as the most productive copper operation in the state during the 1920s, achieving this status in 1929. Situated at a 6,500-foot elevation in central Plumas County, the mine is about 12 air miles east of Quincy. During its two and a half decades of operations, Walker Mine grossed $23 million and had more than 1,000 employees and 3,000 residents during its peak years.

George Bemis made his discovery with local assistance in 1904; however, mining operations did not begin until 1911. Initial yields by 1914 were sufficient to warrant construction of a bunkhouse and three cabins for workers. High-grade ore assaying 12 percent copper was struck in October 1915. A new flotation plant was completed in 1916 with a daily capacity of 85 tons. The mine's sawmill, run by Charles Campbell, was capable of cutting 7,000 feet daily. Electricity arrived in 1917 when a power line was brought from Indian Valley to the mine by Great Western Power Company.

A unique feature of the Walker Mine operation was its 9-mile tramway completed in 1919. It was built to transport copper ore in 3-foot-by-4-foot buckets from the mine to the WPRR siding at Spring Garden. There it was loaded into gondola cars and freighted to Tooele, Utah for smelting. Also transported by the tram during winter periods were food, freight, mail, and occasionally people. The line ran on wooden towers, each from 20 to 60 feet in height. In winter, when the snow was extraordinarily deep, crews were employed near the summit of Grizzly Ridge to shovel the snow out of the line of travel of the buckets.

During Walker Mine's most productive years, it was operated by the Anaconda Copper Mining Company. The company town had a hospital, movie theater, school, dining facilities, store, post office, service station, baseball field, and ski hill. Occupants lived in 132 company constructed homes, 4 bunkhouses of three stories each, and 68 private homes. During its heyday, 75 students attended the school and were taught by three teachers.

Copper prices and yields began dropping, and the company suffered a loss of $300,000 in 1939. The monthly payroll in 1940 for the 325 remaining employees was $75,000. Walker Mine closed permanently in 1941 and was sold at auction in 1945. Nothing but scars and a logged-over bit of rubble remain of this once flourishing town.

Gold was the lure for miners and copper the bread and butter of the mineral industry during the early 1900s. Now little is left of either, only secluded rock piles and overgrown hillside scars.

This c. 1920 hoist man at Engels Copper Mine controlled cables lowering men and equipment into the mine and hauling up the valuable copper ore.

3. CHINESE: PERSEVERANCE EXEMPLIFIED

Chinese made up a significant segment of Plumas County's population from the early 1850s to 1900, particularly during the 1880s. The majority mined for gold, were laborers, or worked as domestic help. A small number of Chinese were in Taylorsville in 1852, digging a water ditch for Jobe Taylor to power his sawmill. At the same time, others were scattered all about the county, digging in streambeds or laboring on ditch construction. Plumas County was the scene of extensive mining activity in the 1850s, but equal opportunity along the hundreds of miles of gold-bearing creeks did not apply to the Chinese. The Chinese generally waited for the white miners to abandon their locations so they could move in. Patiently, they re-worked the same auriferous soil and tailings for overlooked flakes.

American miners were upset with the large number of foreigners working the gold region, and in response, the state legislature passed the Foreign Miners' Tax in 1850. The legislation was directed primarily at the Mexicans and South Americans at first as few Chinese were in the state yet. During 1851 and 1852, however, nearly 45,000 Chinese arrived. Each foreigner had to pay $3 to $4 a month or more, depending upon the year for the privilege of mining. Each county sheriff collected the tax, keeping 20 percent for himself, and each was a conscientious collector. The county and state each received 40 percent. Some dedicated county sheriffs became the highest paid public employees in the state.

The Chinese, taxes paid or not, were forced to confine their activities to non-competitive locations or to re-work abandoned diggings. If these areas proved to be rich, the Chinese were driven out. In Plumas County, the tax was seldom enforced on any foreigner except the Chinese; thus, it was Chinese tax money that contributed greatly to the county's coffers from 1854 until 1870 when the tax was repealed.

Both companionship and a safe home were important to the ostracized Chinese miners. During the mid-1850s, Chinese prospectors near Spanish Ranch found satisfactory returns in diggings abandoned by the whites and founded the small settlement of Silver Creek.

American and Mexican miners had already worked the creek and moved on. The Chinese miners patiently re-worked the abandoned Silver Creek diggings

These young Chinese boys are thought to be from the Moy Foote family of Saw Pit Flat. They would ride their donkeys picking up trash and other articles to sort through and resell. This 1890s photo was taken on the Quincy–La Porte Road near the Thompson Ranch.

for $2 or less a day. These meager returns ensured the Chinese a peaceful place to exist. They were satisfied with the quantity of gold and grateful that American miners and other residents approved of their location.

Other Chinese miners soon learned of their countrymen's relative good fortune and came to investigate, which led to the construction of multiple wing dams upstream. Additional shacks and cabins were erected and, by 1857, the Chinese settlement on Silver Creek was thriving. By the end of the 1850s, Silver Creek had a population of approximately 200, the largest all-Chinese community in Plumas County.

Vegetable gardens were planted and hogs, cattle, horses, and burros were raised. Some residents began a mule pack train business, supplying fresh pork and vegetables to miners along the various Feather River branches and tributaries. Permanent homes, many of them joined together, were erected, replacing the hastily built huts and cabins. A butcher shop and large general store were built. The store was owned and operated by Dick Shoon, who later joined with partner Mun Gee. Gee, whose name was anglicized to "Moon," soon became sole proprietor and conducted a profitable business for many years.

Gee Chin, Sam Wah, Hong Chong, and John High Chan were among those Silver Creek businessmen taxed by Plumas County in 1864. With a net worth of $1,425, John High Chan was judged to be the wealthiest of the Silver Creek citizens.

Economically and socially, the Silver Creek Chinese were content to live a tranquil, segregated existence. An attractive, two-story Joss House was the pride of the settlement. Chinese residents of Plumas County now had a religious and social gathering spot where they could meet for worship and companionship. Tea and rice were everyday staples, with chicken and pork for enrichment. Overall, they were hard working and industrious and soon became the model Chinese town in Plumas County.

The gate to the Chinese town was open to only a select few whites, mostly businessmen. This routine was followed until the arrival of Chinese New Year when a few male Caucasians participated in a time for liquidating debts and meeting friends. During this season, friends in the area were remembered with gifts of Chinese candy, lichi nuts, and jars of preserved ginger. Strings of gaily-colored firecrackers and sticks of punk were given to the children. The women were presented with beautifully embroidered silk scarves or handkerchiefs.

Wishing to return these favors, the Meadow Valley–Spanish Ranch folks would present their Chinese neighbors with gifts of cigars, bacon, ham, headcheese, pickled pigs feet, or beautifully decorated layer cakes and other types of pastry. On such dress occasions, the Chinese men wore silk caps, heavy silk blouses of dark blue or black fashioned with full sleeves extending several inches below their fingertips, and baggy pantaloons and cloth slippers with thick soles.

Moon Key of Silver Creek took advantage of a nice day in 1905 to drive his family into Quincy in his fine buggy. It was unusual for Chinese to own such items as buggies, so this photograph is a particularly unusual one.

The Joss House at Silver Creek, though Western in exterior style, was a religious and social gathering place for Chinese from all over Plumas County. On the second story porch along with "Duke" the dog is seated Bob Bone, a local Caucasian miner. Whites were invited to Chinatown on special occasions such as Chinese New Year.

Chinese hairstyles were unique by American standards. The men's heads were shaved clean except for a round patch about 4 or 5 inches in diameter over the crown of the head. Here the hair was allowed to grow long, then divided into three parts, spliced with heavy silk threads, and then braided together. When working, they usually wrapped these "queues" around their heads or wound them into knots on top.

Greenville, Taylorsville, La Porte, and Quincy each had a Chinatown, while prominent mining centers such as Hopkins Creek, Jamison City, Nelson Point, Sawpit Flat, Mountain House, Rich Bar, and Crescent Mills also had Chinese residents during their heyday and after. At each community, Chinatowns were made up of a few general merchandise stores, a butcher shop, drugstore, barbershop, doctor, saloon(s), opium den, and gambling house. Fan-tan and Chinese lottery were the favorite games of chance. For homes, they usually lived in little shanties, tents, and patched up cabins.

La Porte was a mecca for Chinese occupants; a well-defined community of Chinese resided there by 1858, with males outnumbering females 50 to 1. Few

Robert Moon is shown here with his sister Genevieve Moon Quan. Bob grew up in Quincy, and after serving in World War II earned a degree from San Jose State, then went into the commercial art business and finally returned to Plumas County to serve as Chamber of Commerce manager and first curator of the Plumas County Museum.

arrests were carried out by local peace officers, but when a 21-year-old Chinese woman was kidnapped, the investigation was conducted locally for a month until she was rescued. In various settlements, especially those along main travel routes where hotels were available, such as Summit, Bucks Ranch, Meadow Valley, and Spanish Ranch, Chinese workers were employed as cooks, gardeners, and laundry men.

The combination of Chinese, silk clothing, and a state sericulture subsidy in the 1860s and 1870s led American Valley rancher John Thompson to employ several Chinese to plant mulberry trees. He then imported silkworms to feed on the leaves, hoping to enhance the state's silk and cocoon industries.

James Edwards, proprietor of the Plumas House hotel, tried a similar experiment when he directed "Old Mose," his Chinese gardener, to raise tobacco plants in a section of the hotel's garden plot. After the tobacco had reached maturity, the leaves were dried and made into cigars; apparently they didn't catch on. Neither Thompson's nor Edwards's ideas progressed beyond the experimental phase.

By World War I, productive mining for the Chinese was a thing of the past and most had left for employment opportunities elsewhere in the state. San Francisco was the most attractive, having abundant job opportunities, higher pay, and larger numbers of women. With no ties to hold them, Chinese populations of the various Plumas County towns began diminishing. At Silver Creek, elderly family members and cherished friends began passing away or returning to China. Younger family members were sent away to college for an opportunity to reach their maximum potential and, except for summer vacations, they never came back to Silver Creek.

The Silver Creek population continued to dwindle. Sometime around 1926 the town burned to the ground, including its stores, boarding houses, and the family and single occupancy homes. Only the Moons' home, located about a quarter mile from town, and an old hay barn survived. It was in the Moon family log home, built in the early 1900s, that Bob Moon and his sister Genevieve were born. Their father had died just a week before Bob's birth and, for the next eight years, they lived at their Silver Creek home. In 1934, the family moved to Quincy where uncles Hang and Goon had started businesses. Bob and Genevieve left after high school, but Bob returned in 1960 and became manager of the Plumas County Chamber of Commerce and the Plumas County Museum's first curator.

Dredging operations in the 1930s, followed by tractors and logging, leveled the town, erasing almost all evidence of Silver Creek's once thriving Chinese community. No longer were flowers placed on the 26 or more depressions in the nearby Chinese cemetery. Weeds and pine needles soon covered them and the town of Silver Creek became a memory. A row of tombstone markers in the Meadow Valley Cemetery bearing the names of Gee Moon, his wife Wong Poy Moon, their five sons, and two of their three grandchildren are silent reminders of the Chinese influence on Plumas County. There are just a handful of American-born Chinese in Plumas County today.

This rare interior photo of the Silver Creek Joss House shows cakes and pies given to the Chinese by local housewives for Chinese New Year, 1896. The papers pasted to the beams are good luck banners. The clock on the wall hangs in the Plumas County Museum in Quincy today.

4. AGRICULTURE: SETTLING THE FERTILE VALLEYS

Some of the first ranching in Plumas County is attributed to several Mexicans who came to Meadow Valley in 1850 and claimed the eastern part of the valley. The location where they rented grasslands to miners for their mules became known as Spanish Ranch. The Turner brothers arrived at American Valley in 1850 and claimed all the lands lying south of Spanish Creek. They began charging miners a fee to pasture their mules while they were looking for gold.

George Wangelin was the first rancher to successfully drive his cattle from the Chico area to Plumas County, 57 crooked miles to Bucks Ranch, an elevation of 5,100 feet. Wangelin and five cowboys made the drive repeatedly in six to eight days, allowing for several stops a day to graze. The drives continued for 70 years until Bucks Ranch became Bucks Lake in 1928.

Jobe Taylor's gristmill, built in 1856, provided grain mill service for Indian Valley farmers. Taylor charged 45¢ per bushel for grinding grain and could grind 100 bushels from sunrise to sunset.

Daniel R. Cate, his brother L.F. Cate, and the Judkins brothers were among the first settlers in American Valley. They picked a site at today's Quincy Junction near its intersection with Chandler Road and called it the New England Ranch. It was here that Daniel Cate opened the first store and blacksmith shop in American Valley. During the winter of 1852 and 1853, he constructed the first sawmill along Mill Creek. In the spring of 1853 he went with his brother and E.W. Judkins to the Sacramento Valley to buy wheat, then hauled it back over the Sierra on hand sleds. They sowed 15 acres on their ranch, which yielded 50 bushels to the acre. Much of this was sold for seed in both American and Indian Valleys.

Elijah Poorman located a ranch between today's Quincy High School and the New England Ranch. James Hayes took up the National Ranch, William and Russell Alford started their ranch at Mill Creek, and several others laid out their ranches, claiming most of American Valley.

By 1880, about 20 farmers owned a collective total of 4,500 acres of ranch land, nearly 70 percent of American Valley's 6,720 acres. Beef and dairy cattle, hay, wheat, oats, barley, potatoes, vegetables, and fruit orchards contributed to the ranching way of life. The valley was well favored with three creeks crossing it: Spanish Creek, Spring Garden Creek, and Mill Creek. An 1890 *State Resources* publication described American Valley as "one of the most fertile and lovely of the mountain valleys that are scattered throughout the whole range of the green Sierra."

Twenty miles to the north, Indian Valley's most prolific products were hay and oats, with 8,000 tons of hay being cut in 1876. A new gristmill was built in 1873. Some 500 milk cows enjoyed the native grasses and thousands of acres of clover, as well as the annually planted redtop and timothy. Dairy ranchers found a ready market for their butter at 35¢ a pound; one rancher shipped over 10,000 pounds of butter to Chico via horse-drawn wagons. Indian Valley ranchers were already earning a reputation for their quality horses. On his 160 acres of valley land, Nathaniel Forgay raised a herd of fine horses, plus beef and dairy cattle, sheep, and hogs. He constructed four barns to store his hay for winter feed. The Schaffer Ranch, "one of the most valuable farms in the valley," sold to A.J. Hathaway for $9,000. By 1880, Indian Township's population was 1,712, ranking it as one of the county's most populous. Ranchers included Nicholas Stampfli, Frank Stampfli, Dustin Hedrick, and the Forgays, Bloods, Pulsifers, Schiesers, Smiths, Peters, Hunts, Toscanis, Hickersons, and scores of others.

Dairy ranching was becoming a more common way of life by the turn of the century. It was mainly a family operation: hand milking the cows, hand churning

Dairy herds were an important aspect of Plumas County's agricultural economy. The Italian-Swiss in Sierra Valley developed large dairies, producing enormous quantities of butter, cheese, and milk. Indian Valley dairy herds were also very productive.

The Thompson Ranch off La Porte Road east of Quincy, pictured here c. 1906, grew top quality produce and farm animals of many varieties.

the milk into butter, making cheese, and delivering the butter and cheese by horse-drawn wagons to Chico or Reno.

In 1904, five Taylorsville–Indian Valley dairy ranchers saw the need for a creamery and combined their efforts to open the Taylorsville Creamery to perform the time-consuming hand churning of the milk and delivery to market of their finished dairy products. Soon, 30 nearby ranchers saw the advantage of such an operation and joined the cooperative, most of them becoming stockholders. Elmer Kokem was the creamery's first operator and manager, and was later succeeded by George E. Boyden. In three years, the creamery paid for itself and was averaging a daily output of 600 pounds of butter.

Not only did the creamery ease and enhance the dairy farmers' way of life, a bonus soon appeared in the form of a new cow-milking machine. Frank B. Hosselkus was among those so impressed with the machines that he bought one in 1907, described as follows:

> The machine was provided with two large tubes from the end of which are appended four suction cups, which are placed over the cow's teats. Two cows are milked at one time, the milk being carried through a tube to a pail hung on the machine. Besides having a labor saving's advantage, the machine assures clean milk, there being no opportunity for dirt to get into the pail.

In Genesee Valley, 6 miles east of Taylorsville, the Hosselkus Ranch, Flournoy Ranch, Davis Ranch, and a number of others took advantage of the prime growing and grazing land. Around 1880, a store and stage stop was established opposite the Hosselkus home that is still in operation to this day.

Jonathan Martin came to Big Meadows in 1873, homesteaded 160 acres, and began raising beef cattle and dairy cows and making butter. He purchased 320 acres of range and obtained additional lands under the Swamp and Overflow Land Act, soon increasing his holdings to 1,300 acres. Cutting wild hay for feed, Martin had 100 to 200 head of cattle, plus 35 to 40 milk cows. In 1888, his son Arthur bought the first cream separator in the valley for making butter. Stock cattle from the Sacramento Valley were brought to Big Meadows in 1859 by Peter Olsen, Reuben and Thaddeus Stover, and Melissa Bailey with her husband Jeremiah. Dairying was the leading industry in Big Meadows in the 1860s and 1870s.

Sierra Valley is a large alpine valley in eastern Plumas County. A few Sierra Valley inhabitants took up farm sites in 1852 and 1853, built dwellings, began cultivating their land, and introduced the first cattle to the valley. Their cattle and ranching efforts developed into the second most productive economic activity in the county. Wild grass in Sierra Valley grew as high as a man's head. Winters were harsh, Washoe Native Americans caused problems occasionally, and the lack of good transportation routes made settling the valley difficult. Gradual growth continued and government land laws helped this growth, the Homestead Act of 1862 being the most important.

Bucks Ranch, along the Beckwourth route from Quincy to Oroville, raised cattle and included a large hotel and stage stop.

Nathaniel Strang began ranching in the Sierra Valley in 1856. His 22-year-old son Jared joined him two years later and together they upgraded the cattle business for the area. Jared located a quarter section of land next to his father's holdings and added more over the years. Stock cattle were his primary business, but storing hay for winter feed was equally important. Bunch grass, which produced the finest quality hay in the world at that time, and wild clover grew in abundance in Sierra Valley, while red top and timothy proved equally valuable.

Francis Rowland and George Humphrey also had growing cattle ranches, raised vast quantities of hay to feed their livestock, and made substantial sums of money selling their products to the Comstock Lode and Reno, a town that began in 1862 as a construction camp for the nation's first transcontinental railroad.

Abraham Ede arrived about 1862 when Sierra Valley's population growth began accelerating. Ede combined dairying, beef cattle, and horses on his 200-acre ranch about 4 miles northeast of Beckwourth near the Buttes. Ede's wife kept busy helping her husband drive the family ox team during the day and raising 12 children. A host of others came in the 1860s, taking advantage of the Homestead Act to obtain land and begin beef and dairy ranches: such families as the Bringhams, Rowlands, Speerys, Myers, and Pecks. Isaac Sattley Church from Vermont first settled in Sierra Valley in 1858.

In the Island School District, the grasses were so tall it was said that after turning loose 5,000 head of large Texas Longhorns, "you could not see one of them, but only the man on the horse." Throughout the 1850s and 1860s, there were no fences in Sierra Valley. Longhorns freely roamed the valley floor's common range. By the second half of the 1860s, it became the general practice to drive the herds

Hay was one of the major crops in all the tillable valleys in Plumas County. It was first cut by hand; later horse-drawn mowers made the job a little easier until motorized hay mowers and balers were invented. Most of the hay was stored in barns for winter feed.

Grain crops did well in the fertile valleys of Plumas County. Some crops grew so high you couldn't see a cow standing in them! This photo was taken c. 1900.

during the winter, when the valley floor was covered with snow, into western Nevada, their new range spreading east and west from Reno to Winnemucca, and north and south from Reno–Carson City to Surprise Valley above Alturas. In the spring, bulls, cows, and calves were rounded up and driven back to the Sierra Valley. Calves were branded and earmarked, and each rancher drove his herd home. More ranchers came, bringing more cattle. Fences soon followed and the Sierra Valley's open range became a memory. When the last Nevada roundup was made, more than 200 cowboys returned with 150,000 cattle.

Soon, dairy cattle began replacing the beef stock. Dairy ranching meant more work per cow, but also a higher economic return per animal. The Irish were prominent among those in the development years of the new dairy cattle period in the Sierra Valley. A number had begun arriving during the 1860s, many settling in the central district of the vast valley. Among the Irish were the O'Haras, Gilbins, Sharkeys, Caseys, McElroys, and McCauleys. The Marbles, another Irish family, owned a 437-acre ranch near Beckwourth around the turn of the century. Daughter Alice was born in 1913 and the family moved to San Francisco when she was three years old. Alice soon learned to play tennis at Golden Gate Park and later attained tennis "Hall of Fame" status.

Italian-Swiss immigrants began coming to Sierra Valley as early as 1860, but the period of their greatest influx in Sierra Valley was from 1870 through 1890. Because they arrived later and most of the available land was already taken up, they were forced to purchase land from the earlier settlers. The most common Sierra Valley pattern for land ownership by these immigrants involved three stages: milker, tenant farmer, and landowner. Frank Guidici had worked as a milker on the E.D.

Hosselkus Ranch in Genesee Valley in the 1860s, taking out his pay in cows. A.D. Agostini and Carlo Trosi came in 1874, forming a partnership. Giovanni Dotta settled the same year, following a period of mining at Virginia City and ownership of a Jamison City dance hall. The next year, Frank, Bernardo, and Peter Guidici purchased the 320-acre Stephen Ede Ranch. Emilio Ramelli and Lodovicio Dotta come in 1879 and began operating their dairies as partners. Filipe Guidici settled in 1881 near Vinton and David Ramelli arrived in 1884 near Beckwourth.

Milking their cows, churning their butter, or making cheese, they worked hard and thrived. Every ranch made its own butter and packaged it in 50-pound butter tubs called firkins. These were stacked in their cellars. Cheese was made in large copper kettles suspended over a fire, placed in molds, and aged in the cellar. The cheese and butter were then placed in wagons and transported to Johnsville, Reno, or Virginia City. In 1884, Charles Laffranchini hauled 600 pounds of butter weekly from his Clover Valley ranch to Reno. Dairying was big business for Plumas County settlers in the Sierra Valley. Holstein dairy cattle and Hereford beef stock were introduced in the 1890s, both with considerable success. The Italian-Swiss dairymen often formed business partnerships and married into one another's families or those of other Italian-Swiss ranchers in the Washoe Valley. Their proximity to one another in a foreign country was comforting. They developed a strong sense of community and helped create stable and lasting communities in Chilcoot, Vinton, Loyalton, and Beckwourth. Although the dairies are gone, ranching is still a way of life in the Sierra Valley with many of the original Swiss-Italian families still working the land their forefathers acquired.

Basque sheepherders and their flocks were a routine, seasonal presence, particularly in Eastern Plumas County. They were well known for their delicious breads and unique tree carvings.

5. TRANSPORTATION: THROUGH MOUNTAINS AND CANYONS

Throughout the 1850s, legions of miners, expressmen, and pack trains wore Native American footpaths into single-lane roadways through Plumas County's forests. Ridgeback routes were the easiest to follow. As early as mid-October 1850, the *Marysville Herald* stated that, from Marysville, "good feasible roads are already opened as high as the North Fork of the Feather River." A month later, the citizens of Bidwell's Bar called a public meeting for the purpose of listening to the report of the committee appointed to lay out a wagon road from that place to Rich Bar on the East Branch of the Feather River, and on to Nelson Point. The adopted report stated that the committee had been over the entire trail and "cleared away many impediments and marked it so plain that no man with ordinary capacity could miss it."

Mule train operator Edward McIlhaney was among the many thousands who used the Marysville–La Porte–Onion Valley route, where foot traffic was so busy it was only a matter of time before the path became a road. McIlhaney and partner Charles Thomas built a general mercantile store in Onion Valley in 1850, the only two-story building in the rapidly booming mining town. Things were going so financially well for McIlhaney and Thomas, and the ridge route foot traffic was so heavy, that the pair began using horses and wagons the next year. They hauled passengers and freight from Marysville to Onion Valley, the first wheeled vehicle service in the county.

Another route into Plumas County was by way of 5,212-foot Beckwourth Pass, the lowest mountain pass over the Sierra Nevada. This immigrant route was developed in 1851, a year after its discovery by African-American mountain man James P. Beckwourth. The Beckwourth Trail began near present-day Reno, Nevada, crossed the Sierra Nevada at Beckwourth Pass, continued through Sierra Valley to American Valley, up the mountains to Bucks Ranch, and down the mountains to Bidwell's Bar and the Sacramento Valley. The route was described as "well watered and timbered, with the greatest abundance of grass." Between 1851 and 1854, 1,200 emigrants used the Beckwourth Trail, leading 12,000 head of cattle, 700 sheep, and 500 horses.

By 1853, the Humbug Road had become a popular route from the Sacramento Valley to Humbug Valley and on to Big Meadows. Numerous gold discoveries had led to the development of scattered gold camps. Food and supplies were obvious necessities at the new camps and routes to reach them became priorities. Deer trails and Maidu footpaths had been fine for the earliest prospectors, but wagon roads were soon needed.

At their first official meeting in the fall of 1854, 13 county roads were established by the Plumas County Board of Supervisors. Since the county treasury had no money when the board of supervisors first met, an ordinance was passed to accelerate the mandate for better roads by requiring all able-bodied men between the ages of 18 and 50 to perform three days of labor upon the county road in his district or pay $3 per day missed to the county.

Private enterprise was more effective. In 1855, a toll road was completed from Quincy to Spanish Ranch, bypassing Emigrant Hill above Elizabethtown. Two years later, a second toll road, known as the Pioneer Wagon Road, continued in a westward direction from Spanish Ranch to Bucks Ranch and on to Buckeye near the Plumas–Butte County line, and ultimately to Bidwell's Bar. This road became the heaviest traveled route in Plumas County by the end of the 1850s.

From Bucks Ranch, a large number of miners, merchants, and mule trains traveled north to Rich Bar, Smith Bar, Junction Bar, and other Feather River gold camps. Large numbers of others turned south through Granite Basin to Butte Bar and the numerous mining camps along the Middle Fork of the Feather River. Still others moved on to Meadow Valley, Spanish Ranch, Eagle Gulch, or

To get supplies to the remote mines of Plumas County, pack mules were employed as the most effective, cost efficient method. This string of pack animals is stopped in front of the original Plumas County Courthouse about 1900.

Mountain House, while Elizabethtown or the new county seat of Quincy were the destinations for others.

Mail service was slow and irregular. Winter snows on the high elevation ridge routes meant no travel outside the county, thus no mail for three to five months. Fenton "Buck" Whiting saw the need for regular mail service and began use of a dog-pulled sleigh when the Oroville-Quincy stage had to stop for the winter. Whiting acquired three large dogs that were a "cross between the Alpine Spaniel, or 'Bernadine' and the Newfoundland." Next, he had a bobsled made for $75, harnessed the three dogs in a triangular arrangement, and made his first trial run. In late 1858, Whiting and his dog sled express began hauling up to 500 pounds of mail and freight regularly from the Buckeye Ranch up the mountains along the Bucks Ranch route. One round trip was made per week from Quincy to the valley in two days, with two days to return. Whiting usually traveled at night when the snow was firmer, accompanied by "dog sleigh bells giving him music to enliven his solitary pilgrimages." During a storm, he sent men ahead on snowshoes to keep the trail open. Occasionally, he used four dogs when he had a passenger to ride with the mail.

Seven years was enough for Buck Whiting and his dog team express. In 1865, he replaced his dog team with horses using snowshoes. Square wooden plates were initially placed on the horses' hooves, but damp snow clinging to the wood impeded movement and they were soon replaced by iron shoes. This was an improvement, but still not as smooth and comfortable as desired. Spanish Ranch blacksmith Henry Kellogg remodeled the iron shoes by attaching 9-inch square, thin plates with rubber bottoms. Snowshoe clad horses carrying mail soon began regular deliveries from La Porte to Nelson Point to Quincy, as well as other points in the county. They continued doing so in Plumas County for 45 years, from 1865 to 1910, when mail delivery was assumed by the Western Pacific Railroad (WPRR).

By 1853, Daniel Cate, a successful American Valley rancher, operated a mule pack train business, bringing food, clothes, mining provisions, and other supplies to Plumas County residents. Each round trip made by Cate required 15 to 30 days travel. Richard Irwin of Rich Bar was also a mule pack train operator. Irwin was elected to the state legislature as an assemblyman from Butte County in 1852, reelected in 1853, and then voted into the same office in 1854 by the people of newly formed Plumas County. He ran for lieutenant governor of the state in 1862, but was defeated and retired from politics, living the rest of his life at Rich Bar where he died at the age of 41. He was buried in the Rich Bar cemetery.

Wilson Dean, like thousands of others, used the Lassen Trail to California and mined at Bidwell's Bar and vicinity. By May of 1850, he had $4,000 and moved to Meadow Valley where he bought a ranch and general store. Mule packing seemed to offer a financial potential, so in the fall of 1851, he purchased a train consisting of 45 pack animals, increasing to 90 mules over the next four years. Though not a miner himself, Dean had interests in several mining claims, ran his store, and was selected by the state legislature as one of three commissioners to conduct the legal separation of Plumas County from Butte County and develop an orderly plan for Plumas County's political beginnings.

The mule pack train owners delivering food and supplies from Marysville to Rich Bar used the ridge trail from Bidwell's Bar to Buck's Ranch. So heavily was the route used that, as early as 1851, prospector and mule pack train lodging places lined the entire trail. The eating-lodging sites were located where there was good water and green grass for the mules.

Mill House, 8 miles east of Bidwell's Bar, was the first eating and overnight stopping place; 6 miles farther, the Berry Creek House was known for offering the best of mountain accommodations; 14 more miles uphill and the packers came to Mountain House, a well-known landmark; and 9 miles more was Peavine Ranch, known today as Merrimac. French Hotel, Buck's Ranch, and Meadow Valley were 10, 20, and 30 miles further.

As the mule train neared its destination, shouts rang out: "Pack train coming!" This announcement was further confirmed by the tinkling of bells and the braying of the heavily loaded mules. Upon arrival, the creatures would be unloaded and the muleteer-merchants would display their goods for sale. Traders sold everything from blankets and clothes to food and mining tools. Packers sold their wares using the customary gold exchange rate of 1 ounce of gold for $16 in goods. The packers carried small scales to make their transactions. The "flea market" atmosphere surrounding the mule packers' business provided an exciting diversion. Profits for the packers were large. During the earliest years when all merchandise sold at premium prices, mule train owners charged 75¢ a pound in freight costs and each mule carried 200 pounds of goods. When the pack train owner had 50 mules in his train, in a two week round trip from Marysville to Rich Bar, he could make $7,500, the same amount it took a hard-working miner a year and a half to earn on the streams.

Wilson Dean ran his mule pack train until 1855 and then successfully operated a stagecoach business from Oroville over the ridge trail to Buck's Ranch. The 49-mile trip normally took two days, eating and spending the night at one of the hotels enroute. In 1857, Dean and one of his partners assisted the county in the development of the Pioneer Wagon Road from Meadow Valley to Buck's Ranch. Completion of this final stretch of the road enabled the entire 66-mile stagecoach run from Bidwell's Bar to Quincy to be inaugurated in 1858.

Dean sold his stagecoach business to the California Stage Company in 1858. It was the largest stage company in California. Immediately after the purchase, California Stage began operating three times a week. Each stagecoach was pulled by six horses and accomplished the two-day trip during the snow-free seasons. Stage stations were located 8 miles apart, where the horses were changed. Buckeye was the overnight stop. U.S. Mail and Wells Fargo Express items were carried, as well as passengers and luggage. Later on, the stage made the complete Quincy to Oroville or Oroville to Quincy run in a single long day.

Leaving Oroville at 3 a.m., the stages moved to Bidwell's Bar, crossed the Feather River on a suspension bridge, and moved on to Hart's Mill for breakfast

A horse-drawn sleigh, a buggy, and a horseless carriage converged in front of Clinch's meat market in downtown Quincy c. 1920.

and a change of horses. Zigzagging up the ever-curving mountain road, the stages came to Berry Creek, a mail stop, then on to Mountain House, and up a narrower winding stretch to Merrimac, 33 miles from Oroville where they had lunch and changed horses. Soon they came to Walker's Plains. Then it was on to Letter Box at 6,001 feet where another change of horses was made. The climb continued to Frenchman's Hill, then began the descent to Bucks Ranch and the last change of horses. A short, easy climb of less than 3 miles brought them to Bucks Summit, followed by a steep descent to Tollgate, and finally the level ground of Meadow Valley. Seven more miles and the weary passengers arrived in Quincy. The last Oroville to Quincy stagecoach trip carrying passengers, freight, and mail occurred in August 1911.

The first road construction project with Plumas County money was in 1860 from Indian Valley up the north side of Mt. Hough to connect with the existing American Valley route to that place. Since a substantial number of the construction crew consisted of Chinese laborers, this route was named the China Grade Road.

Plumas County's narrow and winding roads were specified by county ordinance to be 10 feet wide. Turnouts were located along the road to allow approaching traffic room. Bells were required on the lead draft animals to signal approaches on curves. Another necessity on all these pre-automobile roads was grass and water for the freight animals. In general, these dirt roads were rough, with ruts, potholes, rocks, and other obstructions. As time progressed, they were improved and county regulations mandated they be "16 feet wide on the flats and ten feet wide of solid ground on the hills."

"Buck" Whiting's Feather River Express operated from 1858 to 1865 until the advent of the horse snowshoe. Whiting's Express was unique in that he employed three large dogs to pull his sled hauling mail, gold dust, and sometimes passengers over winter snows from Buckeye Ranch to Quincy on the Bucks Ranch Road.

Roads in this region that were constructed between 1859 and 1875 included Sierra Valley to Virginia City, Nevada (1859); China Grade on the American Valley to Indian Valley Road (1860); Red Bluff via Big Meadows to Susanville (1860s); Humboldt Road, from Chico via Big Meadows to Susanville (1860s); La Porte to Quincy (1867); Johnsville to Gibsonville (1860s); Mohawk to Johnsville (1872); Quincy to Greenville, up the eastern side of Indian Creek to Indian Falls, Crescent Mills, and Greenville (1872); and Clover Valley Road from Beckwourth to Genesee Valley (1873).

Beckwourth became the commercial freight center of Plumas County in 1895 when the Sierra Valley Railroad (SVRR) arrived. Travelers and wagon hauling teamsters substantially increased usage of the county dirt roads to and from Beckwourth thanks to the new rail transportation system. Upon completion of the rail line to Clairville in 1896 and Clio in 1903, roads to Mohawk and on to Quincy became the scenes of increased traffic.

What is now a 45-minute drive from Quincy to Beckwourth took eight hours at the turn of the century. Quincy to Mohawk by stage required five and a half hours. To Clio took slightly less than seven. From Quincy to Greenville took five hours.

Augustus Bidwell, Clark Lee, and Dr. Fred Davis, financially capable, progressive Plumas County citizens, decided to participate in the nation's automobile ownership craze. Augustus Bidwell had a family car at Prattville by about 1906; Clark Lee had a White Steamer in Quincy by 1909; and Dr. Davis owned a Maxwell while at Canyon Dam in 1910, which he had driven up from Chico, probably over the Humboldt or Humbug Road.

When Dr. Davis and his wife decided to drive from Canyon Dam to Reno in 1912, they were able to make it in one day, despite having 19 flat tires on the way over. Each flat needed a patch and a hand pump to inflate the tire. Dr. Davis didn't have 19 patches; fortunately, he was wearing knee high rubber boots and had a knife in his pocket when they left their Canyon Dam home. When they reached Reno, he was wearing ankle high boots. Dr. Davis said you were lucky at the time to get 1,000 miles out of a tire.

After the March 1907 flood, Plumas County citizens passed a $100,000 county bond by a convincing 418 to 204 vote. The board of supervisors approved funds right away as a result of the mandate. Seven new steel bridges were constructed, two in Indian Valley and one each in Genesee Valley, American Valley, Spanish Ranch, Mohawk Valley, and Sierra Valley.

Arrival of the WPRR in 1909 and the developing belief that the potential for automobiles would soon enable everyone to participate in the new century's diminishing distances was the talk of the times. Oroville and Chico were just down the mountain if you had a car. Sacramento and San Francisco didn't seem so far away any more. The only problem was that there was no year-round road out of the mountains.

The Oroville–Bucks Ranch–Quincy stagecoach route used for the past 50 years was closed four or more months every winter because of snow. Harley C. Flournoy, Clark J. Lee, and a few others decided to make a horse and wagon trip from Quincy to Oroville through the Feather River Canyon. They used the Utah Construction Company's dirt road hacked into the mountainside during construction of the WPRR as much as possible.

The purpose of the trip was to see if a dependable road really could be built in the Feather River Canyon. The group made it, taking a week to make today's hour and a half drive. It could never have been done prior to the Utah Construction Company's primitive dirt wagon road, but now it could be, Flournoy informed the Quincy and Oroville Chambers of Commerce. Only 13 miles of new road would have to be built. The Plumas County Road Association was organized in 1911 to promote the idea.

By 1919, Plumas County automobile ownership was nearing 100 vehicles. Clamor for paved highways was being echoed across the nation as everyone was realizing that the automobile age had actually arrived. State and federal politicians soon responded financially. California led the call, realizing it had to begin planning for the future. There was no state highway system at all, so in 1909, the legislature passed the first California Highway Act, appropriating $18 million. This was followed in 1915 by the second State Highway Act, with a $15 million appropriation. The federal government joined the automobile popularity craze in 1916 by allotting $85 million for state highways built on a 50-50 state and federal expense-sharing basis.

In 1913, H.C. Flournoy learned of federal plans to build an ocean-to-ocean highway. Flournoy pondered the concept of meshing the Beckwourth Pass–Feather River Canyon–Oroville route into the federal government's plan for the Lincoln Highway. Flournoy was a persistent advocate of the Feather River route, but the best result of his efforts was a State Highway Commission request for Arthur W. Keddie to survey the canyon in 1913 as a possible route from Oroville to Quincy. Despite Keddie's 1913 survey and recommendation, it was announced in 1916 that the Feather River Highway would be routed along the existing Quincy-Oroville Road. Rationale given by the highway commission was that the road already existed; hence, construction costs would be cheaper. The commission ignored the fact that the high elevation ridge route would be covered with snow four to six months of the year. '

In 1917, Governor Stephens traveled to Plumas County to investigate proposed highway laterals firsthand. With the governor were other officials who wanted to examine the area. County Surveyor Keddie took advantage of the situation to drive them to Beckwourth Pass in hopes of convincing the governor and party of the superiority of that route. It didn't work. In 1919, the California Highway Commission reaffirmed their decision and the state legislative road committee approved it, but then at the final session of the committee, a meeting that lasted far into the night, it changed its mind and adopted a Feather River Canyon passage.

Even with the advent of motorized vehicles, real horsepower was sometimes needed,—as in the winter of 1920—to help the mail car along to La Porte.

Things moved slowly, though a survey team did get started. Problems, politics, and bickering continued for several more years. At last, after several disappointing reversals, the State Highway Commission reaffirmed its position and recommended approval of the Feather River Canyon Highway. Legislation was passed, and construction began on July 1, 1928. The state announced the Feather River project was part of its newly passed $53.8 million highway program. Construction money would come equally from gasoline taxes and motor vehicle license fees, with occasional assistance coming from federal appropriations.

Work camps were set up near Oroville to build eastward, at Paxton to build westward, and an "honors" convict camp of about 150 state prisoners was set up at Rich Bar to labor in each direction. A small, mobile convict camp and a free field crew moved as canyon work priorities warranted. On the highway side of the river at Rich Bar, 12 to 15 buildings were erected to house and feed the workers. A camp headquarters, cookhouse, machine shop, and equipment barns were built.

The 1929 stock market crash and depression of the 1930s slowed things down. The state's commitment remained, but new highway financing and work lagged. About 2,800 Californians were given jobs on state highways, thanks to the Works Progress Administration, 150 of them directed to Rich Bar.

Diesel powered shovels removed dirt and rocks to make the 25-foot-wide roadbed. Teams of survey parties and engineers staked the roadbed location and grade. Slides continually caused delays. A series of slides at Arch Rock and Grizzly Dome repeatedly caused holdups, plus an additional $200,000 in expenses.

The most difficult segment was between Cresta and Rock Creek. Survey crews had to hang from ropes, for at Arch Rock and Grizzly Dome the bare granite surfaces extended from the water's edge on slopes ranging from 38 to 60 degrees while rising to heights of 1,000 to 2,000 feet.

Extensive blasting was required to lay the road between the nearly vertical cliffs of the mountain and the river. Three tunnels, the Arch Rock at 300 feet long, the Grizzly Dome at 405 feet, and the Elephant Butte at 1,200 feet, nearly a quarter of a mile, had to be blasted through the solid granite.

In 1935, the State Highway Commission was able to allocate $992,000 to the Feather River Highway project for its 1935 to 1937 construction budget. Contracts were awarded for the construction of bridges, and in the next few years 12 were built, the most spectacular being at Pulga, 170 feet above the river. The most unusual one was at Tobin where the road's bridge goes under the WPRR's bridge. In 1936, the Keddie to Rock Creek section was oiled and a "celebrity trip" was made from Quincy to Oroville, taking the 15 cars two hours.

On August 14, 1937, the Feather River Highway was officially dedicated at Grizzly Dome, the halfway point between Quincy and Oroville. California's governor, several state senators, assemblymen, and dignitaries were among the 1,000 interested attendees who came to drive the new highway and participate in the dedication. Chief Winnemucca came from Nevada, along with 30 Paiute Native Americans who set up tepees and campfires near the west opening of Grizzly Dome tunnel and participated in the ceremony.

The Feather River Highway dream was not only a spectacular construction project, but it also boasted marvelous scenery. About 56 miles of the highway were constructed by convict labor at a cost of $4,887,000, while the other 15 miles, including tunnels and bridges, was completed by private contract at a cost of $1.3 million. The total cost for the 78 miles from Oroville to Quincy was $8,150,000, or $104,500 per mile. Seventy years had elapsed since A.W. Keddie recommended the canyon route for a wagon road; 28 years had elapsed from the first North Fork automobile road meeting in 1909 until the highway's opening in 1937.

In the 1930s, automobile travel from Quincy to Greenville was a combination of twentieth-century automobiles sharing the same winding, one-lane dirt road with large freight trucks and occasionally an old horse-drawn wagon. The road itself along the winding mountain route required alert, conscientious driving. Helen Lawry had fond memories of her summer drives from Quincy in the late 1920s and early 1930s to the Taylorsville Grange Hall. Helen and her friends would enjoy an evening of dancing on the Grange Hall's "spring dance floor" to the music of the Sierra Syncopators, the most prestigious dance band in the county. Driving time for the distance at that time was between two and two and a half hours.

By the early 1930s, the county road department began placing liberal portions of crushed rock and gravel on those sections of the road where shade and snows remained the longest, over bumpy stretches and at sharp curves. Two years after the canyon highway construction began in 1928, the state decided to incorporate the Keddie to Beckwourth Pass to Nevada state line section as an additional part of the state highway system. Gravel was used extensively and dust oiling, a paved road veneer, was added when funds were available. By 1936, a hard surfaced road had been completed from Quincy to Reno.

In 1937, the IVRR was faced with bankruptcy. Engels Mine had closed in 1930 and the principal source of IVRR's funds plunged downwards. In 1937, the IVRR requested that the Interstate Commerce Commission allow them to abandon operations. With Supervisor Branley acting as intermediary, the State of California offered to buy the IVRR. The rails and ties were removed and the new paved road was built right on the roadbed. The primary financial assistance rendered for the Paxton to Crescent Mills segment was a $100,000 road appropriation in June 1940 by the U.S. Department of Agriculture, the road being completed that same year. From Crescent Mills, it was extended to Greenville, Canyon Dam, and Lake Almanor in 1940, being in large part paved by 1941, but not completely finished until 1946. The federal government's expanded commitment to the transportation revolution, the automobile age, and paved roads directly benefited Plumas County. Following completion of the Feather River Canyon Highway in 1937 and blacktop surfacing of the secondary roads by the mid-1950s, Plumas County's transportation network had finally moved into the twentieth century.

Plumas County's first bid at a railroad occurred in the mid-1860s when surveyor Arthur Keddie was employed by the Central Pacific Railroad (CPRR) to survey a possible route across the Sierra Nevada for the nation's first transcontinental line from Sacramento (later Oakland-San Francisco) to Omaha, Nebraska. The route he proposed ran from Oroville through the Feather River Canyon to American Valley and on to Salt Lake City, Utah. The CPRR's "Big Four" rejected Keddie's proposal in favor of the more direct, though much steeper Donner Pass route. Keddie's dream of a Plumas County railroad was thus dealt a seemingly mortal blow.

Still optimistic, in 1867, stock was sold to finance construction of the Oroville and Virginia City Railroad. The Comstock Lode's silver and gold was the obvious attraction, along with the financial support of millionaire Ashbury Harpending. Harpending hired Arthur Keddie to have two or three dozen Chinese laborers grade a right of way through a portion of the Sierra, but it all came to naught in 1871, when Harpending sold to the CPRR at a handsome profit.

From 1869 to 1909, at least a dozen new railroad lines in Plumas County were proposed. Railroad construction in regions near the Plumas County borders gained momentum during the 1870s and 1880s. To the west, the Southern Pacific Railroad (SPRR) was working its way north from Roseville and Sacramento, up the Sacramento Valley toward Oregon. To the east, construction was underway in 1880 for the narrow gauge Nevada & Oregon Railroad from Reno toward Oregon. The line's name was soon changed to the Nevada, California & Oregon Railroad, henceforth called the NCO. One of the NCO's first trains to Reno carried $60,000 in gold bullion from the Plumas-Eureka Mine.

The Sierra Iron Company, holder of supposedly valuable iron deposits in Gold Valley, Sierra County, was next to enter the nation's railway craze. In 1881,

When the Feather River Canyon Highway officially opened in August 1937, locals and dignitaries from all over the state converged at the Grizzly Dome Tunnel near the Butte–Plumas County line to celebrate the auspicious occasion.

it planned a 3-foot narrow gauge line from its iron mines to Mohawk Valley to join its proposed main line from Oroville across Beckwourth Pass to meet the NCO line. The new Sierra Iron & Quincy Railroad hired A.W. Keddie as its chief engineer. Some rights of way were acquired and a little grading was carried out in Thompson Valley, but for all practical purposes, little other work was done except on paper.

Plumas County's first actual railroad line originated in 1885 in the minds of two groups of men, one on the west coast, the other on the east coast. California Land and Timber Company (CL&T) was owned by a group of San Francisco capitalists who owned large tracts of timber in the Mohawk Valley region.

Alexander Agassiz and Quincy A. Shaw, multi-million-dollar Boston investors, also owned vast amounts of Plumas County timberland. CL&T purchased the extensive holdings owned by Agassiz and Shaw in 1886 and began to work on the project Agassiz and Shaw had already partially begun. A rail line would be built from western Nevada and the NCO connection over Beckwourth Pass into Sierra Valley and further west through the forests to Mohawk Valley.

Arthur Keddie was hired to survey the narrow gauge line for the Sierra Valley & Mohawk Railroad (SV&MRR) from Plumas Junction over Beckwourth Pass to

The construction of the Western Pacific Railroad during the years 1905–1909 always drew a crowd when it approached a town. Here, some of the townsfolk of Quincy traveled 3 miles to watch the "gandydancers" do their work.

Mohawk Valley and, eventually they hoped, to Quincy. Construction began for the SV&MRR during the fall of 1885 at an NCO location that became known as Plumas Junction. This site was located a few miles southwest of Hallelujah Junction. By early 1886, the climb westward over Beckwourth Pass was accomplished. From there, the tracks were laid a short distance north of today's Highway 70 and continued west to Vinton, temporarily terminating 9 miles east of Beckwourth near the Buttes. Financial difficulties developed for the CL&T after the tracks had been laid to Vinton and all work stopped. In 1889, the timber company and its railroad were placed in bankruptcy proceedings, and the line lay dormant for four years.

Henry Bowen, San Francisco owner of large timber tracts in the Beckwourth-Portola area, acquired the SV&MRR in 1893. He changed its name to the Sierra Valleys Railroad (SVRR) and renewed construction the following year to extend the line to his timberlands. Beckwourth was reached in 1895 and Clairville in 1896. Clairville became a booming lumber town after the rail line arrived, five sawmills noisily operating by 1900. Bowen purchased two SPRR narrow gauge locomotives and daily train service was soon underway, though there was never any official passenger service.

The SVRR was purchased in 1901 by the NCO, which extended it to the sawmills at Clio in 1903 and eventually to its terminus at Davies Sawmill in Graeagle in 1916. This line operated until it was taken over by WPRR in 1918.

The Boca & Loyalton Railroad (B&L) was built in 1901 and was a 26-mile standard gauge line running from Boca, near Truckee, to Loyalton in Sierra County. To accommodate the logging explosion taking place in Plumas and Sierra Counties, the B&L ran about a dozen spur lines from the main track. From Loyalton additional feeder and spur lines were run to new logging camps in Plumas County.

The first B&L feeder track into Plumas County was laid in 1902, northwesterly through Sierra Valley and on to Beckwourth. At this point, a 3.25-mile line called the Horton Spur was run north to meet the 4-mile narrow gauge spur from Horton's Sawmill at the southern edge of Clover Valley. In the same year, the B&L extended its line west from Beckwourth to what is now Portola.

About 1907, a 2-mile spur was built north along Grizzly Creek to haul logs. Five years later, in 1912, ice from Charles Gulling's 14-acre ice pond became another commodity to haul. Within a decade, Grizzly Creek Ice Company employees annually cut nearly 20,000 tons of ice for WPRR refrigerator cars transporting California fruit and vegetables. The Walker Mine Copper Company also used the Grizzly spur for a brief period. Copper concentrates from their mine on the slopes of Mt. Ingalls were hauled by wagon to the Grizzly spur and the B&L for shipment to the SPRR, then eastward to Utah.

By 1908, the B&L had 56 miles of main and spur line tracks. It had 77 trestles, the largest one being 120 feet long. By the 1910s, however, the area's timber had been pretty well cut over and competition from WPRR, whose line was finished and operating in 1909, forced the B&L into foreclosure in 1918.

With the death of railroad magnate Jay Gould in 1892, his son George Gould inherited the Denver & Rio Grande Railroad (D&RG). Young Gould's lines now stretched from Buffalo, New York to Ogden, Utah. George Gould, with his 10,000-mile railroad domain and millions of dollars, decided to extend his line to the Pacific coast.

Gould's D&RG line didn't have any western connections from Texas to California and competitor E.H. Harriman closed the Ogden–Salt Lake City gateway to young Gould. Prospects for extending his line to the Pacific were bleak since the Atchison, Topeka & Santa Fe Railroad and SPRR occupied southern California, while Union Pacific–Central Pacific Railroad (UPRR) controlled the Oakland–San Francisco terminus. Gould had to disguise his moves to construct a new rail line. He directed the D&RG to be the corporate body to build the Beckwourth Pass-Plumas County segment. D&RG President Virgil Bogue, a former UPRR engineer, oversaw field level and financial operations for Gould.

However, the railroad monopoly wasn't Gould's only problem. Hundreds of Plumas County mining claim holders blocked portions of the proposed route and A.W. Keddie, Walter Bartnett, and others also formed the Stockton to Beckwourth Pass Railroad, which Gould was forced to buy.

On March 3, 1903, the Western Pacific Railway (WPRy) was organized in San Francisco to build a broad gauge line from Salt Lake City to San Francisco. Walter Bartnett became the first president of the WPRy line, though Gould was the dominant figure. Gould directed Virgil Bogue to determine the best route and, using a half-century of Arthur Keddie's survey data, Bogue went to work.

With Oroville's elevation at 170 feet above sea level and Beckwourth Pass at 5,212 feet, and the two locations only 92 airline miles from each other, the entire Butte–Plumas County segment of the rail line could be laid at a 1 percent grade. Also, by laying the track on a 1 percent grade, seldom would the line rise much above the Feather River. With a lower elevation, winter snows would be less of a problem. Gould was finally able to arrange financial support for the WPRy line through bond sales by guaranteeing purchasers that the entire route would be constructed at a 1 percent grade and that no curves would be more than 10 degrees.

Line surveys began in 1903, and due to the rugged nature of the country, surveyors often had to dangle by ropes off steep, granite formations to perform their work. The surveys were completed by 1905 and construction began in May at two locations: Spring Garden for preparation of an immense 7,000-foot tunnel and north of Quincy at Keddie near the present-day Spanish Creek bridge. In September 1905, the Utah Construction Company was awarded a $22 million contract to grade and build the railroad line from Oroville to Salt Lake City.

By the end of October, the 6,002-foot-long Beckwourth Pass tunnel was under construction. The Utah Construction Company sent 22 large steam shovels and 22 "dinky" locomotives to aid in the line's construction. To build the railroad bed, solid granite had to be blasted away and dozens of tunnels had to be driven through hard rock masses. Old mining trails were revived and widened into

For the Western Pacific Railroad to cross the Sierra Nevada on a one-percent grade, the Chilcoot Tunnel had to be blasted under Beckwourth Pass. Because of the work carried on here, the town of Chilcoot came into existence. The work was finished in 1908.

wagon roads for hauling railroad equipment into primitive sections of the Feather River Canyon. By early October, Utah Construction Company had already sublet several contracts and a primitive wagon road was well underway for hauling supplies to the various camps along the line.

Construction was ceremoniously begun at Third and Union Streets in Oakland on January 2, 1906, when the first track was placed and the first spike was struck. A similar celebration took place in Salt Lake City on May 24, 1906, with the laying of the first track in a westward direction. Steam shovels, including one that weighed 70 tons, and dynamite were advantages the WPRy had over earlier railroad construction projects. A series of construction camps was set up between Salt Lake City and San Francisco. From each camp, crews would lay track both east and west to speed the project's completion.

Undoubtedly, the most important construction camp was established in today's Portola. Heavy equipment, rails, supplies, and men could be shipped from San Francisco over the SPRR to Boca, and then on to Portola. First referred to as Headquarters by WPRR, the camp underwent two more name changes before it became Portola.

Laborers represented many races and nationalities. The number of Chinese workers was minimal, but Hindus were numerous, as were Japanese, Italians, and Greeks. By August 1906, about 1,000 men were working between Clio and Beckwourth, and during one period in 1907 nearly 6,200 men were toiling in the Feather River Canyon alone. In all, nearly 9,000 men were employed in building the railroad.

One of the more difficult construction areas was at Spring Garden. To maintain the 1 percent grade, a 7,343-foot-long tunnel had to be constructed. Blasting, drilling, and hauling were carried out 24 hours a day, while a nearby sawmill and electric plant furnished boards, beams, and light. Cave-ins were so prevalent that by 1907, the entire tunnel project was nearly abandoned to seek a less troublesome route. Foremost among the construction problems was the underground stream washing in sand and gravel as fast as it could be removed. So persistent was the stream that all work had to stop until suitable galleries could be erected to diminish the water's underground flow.

For nearly two years, Spring Garden was one of the county's most populous settlements. In December 1908, after 37 months, the Spring Garden Tunnel displayed daylight at each end. By May 1, 1909, the 1.25-mile tunnel, the longest on the entire WPRy line, was finished.

Southeast of Quincy, the nearly 1-mile-long "Williams Loop" had to be constructed. This railroad circle at the north end of Spring Garden Valley was necessary to maintain the grade requirement and to increase the line's elevation by 50 feet in order for the Spring Garden Tunnel entrance to be elevated above Estray Creek's high water mark near its southern portal.

On November 1, 1909, Leonardo Tomasso and his crew of "gandydancers" drove the last spike on the Western Pacific Railroad at the Keddie trestle over Spanish Creek. The only spectators were two local ladies and their children. Official ceremonies took place the next year.

At Beckwourth Pass, another tunnel was necessary to maintain the proper grade. This 6,002-foot tunnel under the pass was the line's second longest. The Chilcoot construction camp was located between the tunnel site and the settlement of Summit. To take advantage of the workers' paychecks, the businesses decided to move next to the railroad construction camp. Three decades later, when Highway 70 was under construction, the whole town moved again to its present site.

Construction hazards were routine, and death common. Precipitous mountainsides, raging rivers, flimsy footbridges, landslides, explosions, and more made construction work a dangerous daily endeavor. Despite the hazards, completion of the railroad was coming to a close. In August 1909, 11 carloads of steel were shipped to Keddie for the trestle to be constructed high above Spanish Creek. Expending extra energy and effort, the 480-foot-long bridge towering 150 feet above Spanish Creek was finished in only a month. By early October, the 1-mile-circumference Williams Loop was also completed.

On November 1, 1909, quite unceremoniously, the last spike was driven near the west end of the Keddie trestle by Italian foreman Leonardo Tomasso. Sitting on a nearby pile of railroad ties was the entire audience, consisting of two charming ladies, Mary Smith and Mary Jane Maxwell Hogan, as well as Mary Jane's two daughters, Aileen and Ida (Billie).

The nation's sixth transcontinental railroad was now finished. Arthur Keddie, at 68 years old, wept as he spoke from the courthouse steps on the occasion of the arrival of the first passenger train in August 1910. The completed railroad consisted of 927 miles of track, 41 trestles, 44 tunnels, a grade of no more than 1 percent, and none of the 385 curves in the 117 miles between Oroville and Portola exceeding 10 degrees.

By formal opening day on July 1, 1911, the WPRy had 115 locomotives and a property value of $162 million. Unfortunately, freight revenues and passenger traffic income were well below expectations from the very beginning. Gould was also experiencing financial losses on his eastern rail lines, causing him to default on his bond payment obligations and forcing him into receivership. In June 1916, the WPRy was sold at an auction. Bondholders of the line decided to assume management of the operation themselves, using the name Western Pacific Railroad Corporation.

New WPRR President Charles Levey decided an important reason for the company's financial problems was a lack of feeder lines. He built a 1-mile spur from Blairsden to the Graeagle sawmill in 1916 and purchased the B&L at a foreclosure sale for $35,100 the same year. The newly acquired line became known as the "Loyalton Branch." In 1917, WPRR and Engels Copper Mine jointly financed and built the IVRR from Paxton to Engel Mine in the North Arm of Indian Valley. That same year, the "Plumas Branch" of the NCO from Plumas Junction to Clio was purchased. A year later, WPRR purchased the southern portion of the NCO's narrow gauge line from Reno north to the WPRR main line, soon changing it to a standard-gauge line. In 1923, they built a new Calpine

In late July 1931, this California Fruit Exchange logging train was headed to a logging camp near Calpine when it plunged through the Willow Creek Trestle near Clio. Of the 50 men aboard, 17 were injured, 2 seriously. Within weeks the line was back up and running.

Branch from near Beckwourth, roughly paralleling present-day Road A-23 through Sierra Valley to Calpine.

When Arthur Curtis James acquired control of WPRR in 1926, expansion continued. Since James already had control of the Great Northern Railroad in Washington and Oregon, he decided to construct a north-south "inside gateway" line connecting the Great Northern with the WPRR. A 112-mile extension was made by WPRR from Keddie and an 88-mile southern extension was made by Great Northern from Klamath Falls, Oregon, the lines meeting at Bieber, California. Now the WPRR could compete against the SPRR to carry freight between the Pacific Northwest and California. Called the "High Line," it was appropriately commemorated in November 1931, with president Arthur James driving the gold final spike at Bieber.

Following World War I, prosperity and newer equipment came to WPRR. Business was going so well that 2,000 new refrigerator cars were purchased to serve fruit growers and shippers of other perishables.

However, the Great Depression took its toll, and by 1935 the WPRR was forced to default on its bond interest and was bailed out by the government's Reconstruction Finance Corporation. But even this regressive move was only temporary. While still in receivership status, 700 miles of new rail were laid on the main line.

With the outbreak of World War II, freight traffic more than doubled in 1942 and continued to increase. Soon the company emerged from its receivership and its $38 million debt and even began paying dividends. The number of freight cars increased from 7,000 in 1940 to 8,000 during the war and locomotive numbers grew from 169 to 176.

Diesel engines were introduced in 1939 when three switcher models were purchased from American Locomotive Company (ALCO). In 1941 and 1942, 18 freight locomotives were also purchased. Following the war, Harry A. Mitchell became WPRR's new president. Mitchell decided to phase out the whistling steam engines and "Old Number 37" puffed up its last smoke in 1951 at the Portola train yard as it began its final run to Oroville.

The California Zephyr began operations in 1949 and was the nation's newest passenger train, transporting travelers from Chicago to Oakland in 49 hours. The Zephyr was also the finest of the nation's passenger trains, offering deluxe service and accommodations for less than $50. In 1970, the Zephyr was discontinued due to heavy expenses, increased competition of automobiles, and more affordable airline service. Today, the main line and High Line cater only to freight and are under the ownership of UPRR, which acquired them in 1982 with the collapse of WPRR.

Quincy Western Railway (QWRy) was built in 1910 to connect the town of Quincy to the WPPR's transcontinental line. The little 5.33-mile QWRy standard gauge line was built at a total cost of $80,000, all the money coming from local people. From its depot on Railway Avenue in Quincy, it heads across American Valley to the WPRR tracks at Quincy Junction. The original names of Marston and Hartwell Station were changed in 1915 to Quincy Junction at the request of the chamber of commerce.

Lumber shipments were the QWRy's primary source of income. Petroleum products tankers and small freight shipments were additional sources of revenue. A 37-ton ALCO steam engine pulled a single combination passenger-baggage car and flat cars loaded with lumber. This engine was replaced in the 1930s by 60-ton steam engine Number 2 and by a 44-ton diesel electric unit in 1945.

After a variety of crises, foremost of which was financial, QWRy sold out to the Quincy Lumber Company in 1917, when it was renamed the Quincy Railroad Company. The lumber company, owned by F.S. Murphy, sold to C.A. King in 1937, who then sold in 1956 to the Meadow Valley Lumber Company. The railroad, still known as the Quincy Railroad Company, is now owned by Sierra Pacific Industries.

The development of Engels Copper Mine in the early 1900s resulted in a joint Engels-WPRR construction project, tracks being laid in 1917 from Paxton and the WPRR to Crescent Mills, Veramont (near Taylorsville), and up the North Arm of Indian Valley to the Engels Mine. Indian Valley Railroad (IVRR) was the name given the new line and copper was its primary freight. Just one passenger car, complete with seats and a wood stove, was part of each run. It operated regularly from September 1917 until 1938, traveling a distance of 21.5 miles.

The copper ore was transferred to a WPRR train and carried to a smelter plant in Garfield, Utah. IVRR and WPRR jointly built the Feather River Lodge and a train station at Paxton, as well as an electric light plant, eight bunkhouses, and a few cottages.

The IVRR's engines consisted of locomotives Number 1 and Number 2, a passenger car, freight cars, and a steam shovel. The running time from Paxton to Engels Mine could be accomplished in 40 minutes, but with two stops, the actual time on the run was 2 hours and 15 minutes.

The IVRR initiated line abandonment procedures in 1937, seven years after the closing of Engels Mine. With the advent of the WPRR's High Line, IVRR revenue losses were mounting. The Feather River Canyon Highway was finished in 1937, and the California State Highway Department wished to purchase the Paxton to Crescent Mills portion of the IVRR, scrap it, and build a new highway over its roadbed. Interstate Commerce Commission approval was granted and the IVRR ended.

Today, the only operating rail lines in Plumas County are the UPRR, the Quincy Railroad Co., and the Collins Pine Almanor spur.

The famous Keddie Wye where the high line heads north from the main line was the site of the Ruby Jubilee, a 40th-year celebration of the railroad's completion in 1909.

6. TIMBER: THE BITE OF THE LUMBERMAN'S AXE

J.B. Batchelder erected the first sawmill in Plumas County at Rich Bar on the Middle Fork of the Feather River. His specialty was lumber for the flumes and wing dams the miners were building in the river, but he also cut lumber for frame homes and businesses. His sawmill operated for a decade until the brisk placer mining along the Middle Fork slowed down.

D.L. Pent followed Batchelder's example and erected a sawmill at Nelson Point in 1851. Several others were built in 1852 at Rich Bar on the East Branch of the North Fork of the Feather River. Mineral discoveries elsewhere resulted in the growth of many new mining towns, and sawmills were necessary there also. By 1856, a mill was operating at Mountain House above Meadow Valley. Others built in the 1850s were one at Independence Bar on Nelson Creek and two at Willow Creek in the Bucks Lake–Middle Fork region. In 1860, Indian Valley resident Charles H. Lawrence built a mill at Round Valley. Two years later, Daniel Cate erected a steam mill at the same location to furnish the lumber for that rapidly growing mining town. A primitive whipsaw operation was set up at Sawpit Flat near Onion Valley during that mining camp's early years.

Sawmills continued to provide support to the mines throughout the rest of the nineteenth century at such locations as La Porte, Wolf Creek–Greenville Mining District, and Plumas-Eureka Mine. Sturdy wooden posts were used to shore up mine tunnels and made lumber mills an essential part of the county's gold mining history. Townspeople and farmers also needed lumber products.

Daniel Cate built the first overshot wheel sawmill in American Valley in 1852, along with partners E.W. Judkins and J.S. Boynton. John Hartwell purchased the Cate & Judkins Mill in American Valley, which he operated in the 1860s and 1870s. Pioneer settler Jobe Taylor built a mill in 1855 on his Indian Valley ranch, which he continued to operate until his death in 1878. Taylor's sawmill was powered by diverting water from Indian Creek through his millrace. Taylor constructed the mill so that he could operate it alone. From his millpond 150 feet away, logs were winched into the mill. The saw worked similar to a whipsaw, in an up-and-down manner.

These fallers are shown in the process of falling a large sugar pine with a handsaw or "misery whip" and axes. Along with their faithful companion, they have an assortment of wedges, axes, a shovel, and iron bars. It could take experienced loggers like these about 2 hours to fall a tree this size.

Most of the earliest Plumas County sawmills were built on land next to a creek or river, water from the flowing stream providing the power for the saws to cut the logs into lumber. Logging at first consisted of very small local industries; the wood was mostly worked by hand, with four to eight oxen, mules, or horses pulling logs cut from nearby timber stands to the mills.

Richard Jacks built a sawmill in Meadow Valley in 1854 and Robert Penman and George Woodward built another the following year in Mohawk Valley to satisfy the needs of farmers. In 1858, James Walleck erected the first mill in Big Meadows for bridge construction. By the end of the decade, there were a total of 18 sawmills in Plumas County. About half were in the valleys and half in the mining regions. Daily capacity for these mills ranged from 2,000 to 4,000 board feet a day.

The county's population remained stable during the 1860s, with local lumber needs less than those of the 1850s. With a slowing of business, some mills closed down permanently. By the end of the decade the number of mills dropped from 18 to 10.

During the 1870s, the population increased 28 percent, from 4,489 people to 6,180. Hydraulic mining was instrumental in creating the increase in people and the subsequent increase in the number of homes and stores built in Quincy, La

Porte, and the North Fork–Caribou regions. Quartz mining yields resulted in a similar need for lumber at the Plumas Eureka Mine and in the Greenville area. Charles H. Lawrence built a sawmill in Greenville in 1870 that was soon followed by the Hough's new mill at Greenville's Chinatown and the Schaffer brothers' operation on Wolf Creek.

To the east, a steady growth in the number of Sierra Valley cattle ranchers and farmers created a demand for more lumber for homes, barns, and fences, hence the Otis and Mayne Mill was constructed a few miles east of Beckwourth in 1872. In 1868, Florian Gansner purchased an old mill 1 mile west of Quincy along the Meadow Valley Road, which he operated for ten years. In 1877, he constructed an impressive new mill that was powered by a 144-foot fall of water and for 30 years or more, was considered one of the finest mills in this part of the Sierra.

Accompanying the population increase of the 1870s was an increase in production from the ten county mills. Three mills went up in Mohawk Valley in the 1870s in response to settlement there. By 1882, of 11 sawmills, four were operated by steam and seven by waterpower. Local mills were able to respond adequately to local needs. However, the demands of the fast-growing towns of Sacramento and Marysville for lumber from the Sierra were never-ending. The western areas of Plumas County were the first to answer the calls for lumber products by outside markets. Beginning as early as 1856, above Bidwell's Bar, timber was cut and floated at high water all the way to Sacramento.

Falling timber may or may not have gotten easier with the invention of the gasoline-powered chainsaw. These fallers are using one of the first of these models, equipped with wheels, in the pine stands along the edge of Sierra Valley in 1935.

Virginia City, Nevada had no trees, but did have lots of gold and silver. Lake Tahoe–area timber was its main source during the 1860s and after, but Plumas County also supplied timber to the mines. It was a several-day trip by horse and wagon from the Plumas woods to the Comstock Lode, but for the resolute logger, it could be worth it. So insatiable was the Comstock's need for beef and lumber that the town of Summit on the west side of Beckwourth Pass sprang up in 1859 in response to the traffic going to Virginia City. C.T. Adams erected the Summit House hotel in 1859. In 1862, the stone and mortar Martin Store was opened by George Martin.

Two significant events occurred in the timber industry during the last three decades of the nineteenth century: first was an increase in private ownership of Plumas County timberland and second was improvement in logging and transportation methods. Narrow gauge railroads and wooden flumes provided timber operators a way to move logs from the woods to the market. Timbermen with vision recognized the potential of the stands of timber with the advent of railroad construction in the region.

V-shaped wooden flumes were introduced to the area in 1870. They required less lumber to build, having two sides rather than three, and were easier and quicker to build. The first V-shaped flumes used in Plumas County in 1870 proved extremely successful. One enterprise was a 30-mile-long flume built by Kellum Powell and partners. Constructed of 30-inch wide planks 16 feet long, it made a continuous downward slope of 27 feet to the mile. Immense trestles up to a quarter mile long crossed 100 feet above yawning canyons. Construction costs were $1,500 to $2,500 per mile. Men were stationed at intervals to prevent the lumber from jamming the flume.

The Sierra Flume and Lumber Company, headed by wealthy Virginia City mining financier Alvinza Hayward and lawyer Norton Parker Chipman, was one of the first corporations to exploit Plumas timber stands. The huge stands of sugar pine in the Big Meadows area of northern Plumas County were where they directed their attention. A contemporary lumberman noted it was "the finest timber land in the county."

Extending their claims beyond the Big Meadows area, Hayward and Norton ultimately claimed 80,000 acres of land in Plumas, Lassen, and Tehama Counties. As many as 50,000 acres were claimed around Stover Mountain, Chester, and Big Meadows.

Growth of the Sierra Flume and Lumber Company was extremely rapid. Within two years, the lumber company had ten sawmills in operation cutting an estimated 400,000 feet of lumber daily. It owned 156 miles of flumes; 23 miles of logging tramways; 3 planing mills; 2 sash, door, and blind factories; 250 miles of telegraph lines; and a San Francisco main office and export agency. Plans were in the works for a 49-mile mammoth flume to transport timber from Lost Creek, Soldier's Meadows, and their Big Meadows sawmill, following the Deer Creek route to the Sacramento Valley. All the mills and flume lines were linked by telegraph lines to the company's area headquarters at Red Bluff. It was the largest

Steam powered donkey engines were fueled by wood scraps. They tore the woods apart and were the cause of many forest fires due to sparks from their smokestacks. A seven-man crew was needed to operate these machines efficiently. This photo was taken c. 1911.

private communications network in the state, possibly in the entire United States. Over 43 million board feet of lumber was cut and sold during their first year of operations in 1876; 50 million feet were produced in 1877, sales being made as far away as New York, South America, Australia, and Asia. It was a grand beginning, but despite Hayward's wealth, the Sierra Flume and Lumber Company went bankrupt in 1878.

While bankruptcy of the company in 1878 signaled its ultimate collapse, a new enterprise known as the Sierra Lumber Company picked up many of the pieces that same year. In 1902, the company sold 65,000 acres of its Big Meadows land to timber baron T.B. Walker. This Plumas County tract later became the heartland for the Red River Lumber Company.

From 1850 to 1900, men using single-bit axes, two-man saws, and oxen, mules, and horses provided the timber for the operation of dozens of small sawmills. Oxen and horses dragging logs on skid roads was one of the earliest methods used by lumbermen to move logs to the sawmill. Ten-foot-long, 12-inch-diameter logs were placed in 6-inch deep excavations 7.5 feet apart, resembling railroad ties. The logs were placed such that a 16-foot log, which was the shortest standard length into which buckers would cut the fallen trees, would always lie on at least two of the skid road logs for stability. "Bucking" is the sawing of a tree into logs of standard lengths.

The forward end of each log was trimmed along the edge by an ax for easier dragging. The rounded tops of the half-buried skid logs were swabbed with grease

Horse-pulled "big wheels" lift the weight and drag huge lengths of cut timber to landings, from where they are hauled to the mill.

or tallow, usually by a "greenhorn," new to woods work. After 1900, horses were generally used instead of oxen to pull the logs down the skid road, as a 12-horse team was faster and easier to handle.

Bill McKenzie, the McNair brothers, and Captain John Roberts were early Mohawk Valley lumbermen. McKenzie owned a circular sawmill in Mohawk Canyon north of Calpine and periodically hired the McNair brothers to fall and buck timber for him. Using log chutes (two sets of logs laid parallel to each other for a distance) and oxen, the logs were skidded to a landing. Normally, the cutting was done before winter and the logs moved to a landing to await snow. When the snow was 6 to 8 inches deep, six-horse teams pulled double sleds loaded with logs to the mill. McKenzie's crew could usually pull 700,000 to 800,000 board feet of logs from the landing to the sawmill by Christmas.

The McNair brothers owned and operated a circular sawmill near Calpine from about 1890 to 1915. Among their customers was the NCO, for whom they hauled their lumber over Beckwourth Pass to their line in Long Valley, west of present-day Highway 395.

E.S. Collins, D.G. Curtis, and Charles H. Holbrook of San Francisco, making up the firm of Curtis, Collins, and Holbrook, made a 13,000-acre forest reserve "in lieu" acquisition, 20 miles west of present-day Lake Almanor. The Management Act of 1897, a rider to the 1891 Forest Reserve Amendment, authorized owners of unpatented lands within other forest reserves anywhere in the nation to exchange their tracts in lieu of an equal amount of vacant land elsewhere. This resulted in much cut-over land being exchanged for virgin timber.

No United States land offices were located in Plumas County at the turn of the century, but there were offices in Marysville and Susanville. Land fraud investigator Horace Stevens examined the 1878 Timber and Stone Act entries made during a nine-month period when he visited Susanville in 1902, where a significant amount of the land applied for was in Plumas County. The 503 applications accounted for more than 80,000 acres; "in lieu" acquisitions exceeded even this at 108,425 acres. More than 250,000 acres of Susanville land office timberland was obtained by lumbermen as a result of the "in lieu" and Timber and Stone Act legislation.

In 1902, New York capitalist W.E. Wheeler sent his agent Jacob Cook to northern California where Cook filed on behalf of Wheeler for more than 112 quarter sections (28 square miles) of timberland in southwest Plumas County on each side of the South Fork of the Feather River.

T.B. Walker also took advantage of the "in lieu" legislation. Of the 170 "in lieu" land transactions made at Marysville between 1897 and 1902, 160 were made on behalf of Walker, amounting to more than 26,000 acres. Walker also brought "dummy entrymen" from the east to grab up additional chunks of timberland to then sell back to him. Walker alone owned more than 500,000 acres of California timberland.

The narrow gauge SV&MRR, built in 1885 almost to Beckwourth from Long Valley, was substantially financed by the California Land and Timber

These logs are bound for J.C. Knickrem's Mill near Mohawk, about 2 miles west of Graeagle. Knickrem came to Mohawk in the 1880s and established his family there, some of whom still live in Plumas County.

Company of San Francisco. They built sawmills on their timber lands at Kirby, near Beckwourth, and at Mohawk, the latter mill cutting 15,000 to 20,000 board feet of lumber a day in 1886. Financial problems in the early 1890s stopped westward extension of the railroad; in 1894, the SV&MRR was sold to capitalist Henry Bowen, who renamed it the Sierra Valleys Railroad (SVRR) and extended it to Clairville.

Clairville became a very important sawmill town by 1900. The new town was settled in 1895 in a virgin forest where the SVRR line ended, about 8 miles west of present-day Portola. Clairville was named after one of Henry Bowen's two daughters, Claire, as was Vinton, formerly called Cleveland. A post office was established in 1896 and houses sprang up. Chinese domestic workers arrived and established a Chinatown, and lots were selling for $25 and up. A few dozen housewives and children soon arrived, necessitating construction of a schoolhouse, a grocery store, and other amenities, although the rough, masculine element still predominated.

By 1896, the Clairville Hotel was a very busy place, with drinking, gambling, prostitution, and barroom brawls common. The hotel burned down in October 1898, killing five, but a new two-story hotel quickly replaced it.

The Totten Mill was operating in the area during the 1880s, and two or three other sawmills had been set up by 1895. Within a 10-mile radius of Clairville, thousands of trees were cut and transported to the sawmills. By 1906, the town had one grocery store, one hotel, two barbershops, numerous restaurants, and ten saloons. That same year, the new WPRR line had approached within a mile or so of Clairville. The Utah Construction Company used the town as a construction camp location for the line's 400 to 500 laborers, injecting life into its economy.

By 1907, however, most of the trees were gone and the WPRR line had moved on to a new construction camp at Portola. As Portola grew, Clairville declined. Its sawmills closed and workmen left. By late 1907, Mr. Perry, the grocery store owner, said his wife and one other woman were the only females in town, not counting the 20 or so "camp follower" types scattered among the 16 saloons and red-light houses. The post office was discontinued in 1910 and houses were soon vacant. Heavy snows during the winter of 1913 and 1914 caved in roofs and soon Clairville became a ghost town.

In 1901, the NCO purchased the SVRR and began extending its tracks from Clairville to Clio and Mohawk Valley. This allowed timberland owners to significantly increase their timber cutting activities. The J.C. Knickrem Mill near Mohawk Valley annually turned out thousands of feet of first class sugar pine, the mill cutting 15,000 board feet every ten hours.

About 1900, timber cutting began in an area 7 miles north of Beckwourth in Horton Canyon at the southern edge of Clover Valley. The Horton brothers began purchasing government land and conducting logging operations, and by 1892 had already built a sawmill to take advantage of the recently established SV&MRR. An 1896 report stated that Horton Brothers had 1 million feet of logs in their yard, most of which would be converted into box material for fruit shipping. Fruit

Donkey engines powered the "jammer," which straddled the tracks and was obviously capable of lifting even heavier loads than the huge logs it placed on waiting railcars, c. 1915.

boxes were being made at their box factory, which was established that same year. The Hortons also erected a mill at Beckwourth, adjacent to the SVRR line. In 1900, they purchased a Best Traction Engine to haul logs from Horton Landing to their mill at Beckwourth, possibly utilizing the first motorized logging equipment in Plumas County.

Horton Brothers entered into an agreement with B&L to run a standard gauge spur line halfway from Beckwourth towards Horton's sawmill and the edge of Dotta Canyon. The Hortons would build a rail line the rest of the way to their operations. The Horton half was narrow gauge, with a 12-mile extension constructed in 1907 and 1908 along the base of the hills in Clover Valley.

The Reno Mill and Lumber Company began acquiring significant amounts of Plumas County timberland during the last half of the 1880s, concurrent with construction of the SV&MRR. By 1889, Reno Mill and Lumber owned 7,000 acres of timberland and had a bandsaw mill at Beckwourth cutting 60,000 board feet per day. In May of 1902, a local newspaper described the Reno Mill and Lumber Company's process of bringing its logs from the stump to the three-

The McGiffert jammer loads a Marsh Lumber Company train in Clover Valley c. 1915.

story bandsaw mill located 3 miles west of Beckwourth along the SVRR line. The logs were pulled along a skid trail to the head of a 2.5-mile wooden chute by a ten-horse team. They were then rolled into the chute, dogged together end to end, and then pulled by ten more horses along a parallel tow path, similar to canal barge tow paths. At the end of the chute, another ten-horse team hauled the logs over a skid road to the mill. Reno Mill and Lumber Company estimated the cost was $3 per thousand board feet to bring the timber to the sawmill, while they sold their lumber for $10 per thousand feet. Sawdust was used for creating steam power for the mill.

The Feather River Lumber Company purchased all but 1,000 acres in the Grizzly Creek section, as well as town site property in Portola from the Reno Mill and Lumber Company in October 1911 and built a sawmill in 1914. Jorgenson, Turner, and Fierl of Portola started the Beckwith Peak Lumber Company in 1917, with timber to come from their extensive holdings in the area.

The Plumas County timber industry was given a major boost when the WPRR was finished in 1909. With the arrival of the WPRR, Plumas County timber replaced gold as the county's principal industry. Nine or ten standard and narrow gauge railroad lines worked their way from the sawmills into the forest.

The Clio Lumber Company's narrow gauge line was powered by a Shay geared locomotive, which ran from 1907 to 1914, eventually coming under the control of the Graeagle Lumber Company. This spur line branched from the old SVRR line, which had been acquired by the NCO in 1901.

The Delleker Mill, built in 1905 by Feather River Lumber Company, sat about 2 miles west of Portola and operated for 47 years, until 1954. From the WPRR main line in 1915, the Feather River Lumber Company ran a spur line north from Delleker into the mountains toward the site of present-day Lake Davis. This 30-mile narrow gauge extension was used from 1915 to 1943, so productive was the region's forest.

Another great boost to the timber industry was the steam donkey engine. Steam donkeys soon became the greatest woods production machines in the logging industry's history. Although invented in 1881, for unknown reasons it did not appear in Plumas County until almost 30 years later. First note of its presence in the county was at the White Pine Lumber Company's operation at Cromberg in 1910, where they had a crew of 200 men and 5 donkeys. Basically, the donkey was a semi-stationary, wood-fired, steam-powered engine with a winch. Each donkey sat on a pair of huge wooden runners, called donkey sleds. Engine power varied from 50 to 75 horsepower. On the sled was a large, 2,000-pound iron drum wound with 1,500 feet of cable. A smaller straw line on another drum pulled this cable, or haul line, from the donkey to the logs. Chokers were fastened around the logs by choker setters and then attached to the hook at the end of the haul line. A signal was given to the "whistle punk," who blew another signal, informing the donkey operator that all was ready. The donkey operator blew his warning whistle, then using a set of gears, the haul line began pulling the huge logs toward the donkey, battering or uprooting whatever was in the way.

Each donkey required about a seven-man crew: the donkey operator, a fireman, a woodcutter, a couple of choker setters, a hooker, and a whistle punk. Donkeys were mobile by virtue of attaching their cables to strong trees or stumps and winching themselves from one point to another. They were also small enough to be transported to new sites on log trains.

Horse-drawn "big wheels," two wheels 10 to 14 feet in diameter with 18 to 20 spokes, were mounted on a 6-foot axle. Perpendicular to the axle was a tongue, extending rearward and above the log. The big wheels were jockeyed into a position straddling a log, which was then chained to the tongue. When the horses pulled, the front of the log was raised from the ground, making it easier to pull. Big wheels proved very effective for moving logs short distances and were used for several decades, from about 1890 to 1920 until the successful takeover by Caterpillar tractors in the 1920s and 1930s. For a short period tractors took over for horses pulling the big wheels.

Charles Campbell and Frank Meyers of Beckwourth and Harry Turner of Sattley joined as partners in the new Sloat Lumber Company in spring 1912. The mill started operation in June, cutting an average of 35,000 board feet of lumber per day. By fall of that year, family houses, bachelor cabins, and a boarding house had been built and a railroad depot was erected. In 1915, the Sloat post office was opened. In 1918, F.S. Murphy bought out the Sloat Lumber Company and replaced the mill's circular saw with a band saw. Next, he added a new planing mill and followed that up with a 3-mile, 30-inch narrow gauge railroad. Sloat proved to be an ideal sawmill site, operating for more than 75 years until the mill closed down in 1991.

The Spanish Peak Lumber Company in Meadow Valley was organized in 1915 and began cutting timber the next year. To send rough-cut lumber to their planing mill, an aerial tramway was built a little over 5 miles to Gray's Flat, on the East Branch of the Feather River. The lumber company built a manufacturing plant close to the WPRR tracks with a planing mill, dry kiln, and box factory.

On September 29, 1916, operations began and so successful was the tramway it continued to be used until 1939. Bundles of lumber moved out every three minutes at a speed of approximately 414 feet per minute. Over the 23-year period, more than 250 million board feet of lumber was transported by tram at a cost of around $2 per thousand. A $95,000 investment, it proved to be a profitable operation. Another unique aspect of the Spanish Peak Lumber Company was their change from log trucks in 1926 to a narrow gauge railroad, then back to log trucks in 1933.

Not as spectacular as the Spanish Peak tramway, but of equal value to the industry, was Plumas County's first dry kiln, introduced by F.S. Murphy at Quincy in 1922. Prior to its erection, up to eight weeks were required to dry cut lumber. Murphy's new kiln could dry up to 25,000 board feet per day by directing a blast of hot air upon the lumber, keeping it at an even temperature until the moisture was removed from the wood.

Large logs loaded onto trucks wend their way to the sawmill along the many miles of forest roads in Plumas County. This load of logs was photographed in the 1950s.

90

The Clover Valley Lumber Company, formed in 1915, built its mill in Loyalton to process timber cut in the surrounding area and to utilize the B&LRR services. After the local timber supply was exhausted, the company decided to transfer operations to Clover Valley. After debating the merits of building a new mill in Clover Valley versus usage of its Loyalton sawmill, the company decided to keep the mill and use railroad transportation to Loyalton.

Beginning in 1917 and continuing through the 1930s, Clover Valley Lumber constructed about 60 miles of track north of Beckwourth to Clover and Squaw Queen Valleys. As the merchantable timber was cut around each logging camp, the railroad line was extended and the crews and buildings moved on to the next site. This was done 13 times, the last camp being in Squaw Queen Valley, more than 50 miles from Loyalton. Clover Valley Lumber Company eventually exhausted the timber supply and sold out to Feather River Lumber Company in 1956. Still visible are the remnants of the old roadbed and a few rusty spikes.

The largest Plumas County logging operation up to World War II was the Red River Lumber Company. Established in 1912 as Walker Camp, it soon acquired its present name of Westwood. Westwood is actually located in Lassen County, 3 miles from the Plumas line, but the majority of Red River's operations were in Plumas County.

Red River Lumber Company cut its first tree on September 10, 1912. A small, portable mill was installed first and a large band mill quickly followed. The first full season of logging began in 1913 and continued for three decades with a force of 50 men. Horses and 14-foot big wheels were the primary log haulers in the early Red River days. A crew of three men with their horses and big wheels once delivered 35,000 board feet of logs to the mill in one day. Always looking to improve logging methods, Walker introduced donkey engines in 1914.

Although the WPRR tracks were only 40 miles away at Paxton in the Feather River Canyon, Walker cut a five-year contract with SPRR to ship his logs. A subsidiary line called the Fernley & Lassen Railway constructed a 135-mile line from Fernley, Nevada through Susanville to Westwood. The line, begun in 1912, was completed in the spring of 1914. Red River began using trains by 1915. The first of five Shay locomotive engines, varying in weight from 60 to 150 tons each, arrived that same year. From the main line, feeder lines branched out in numerous directions from which more spur lines a mile or so in length emanated. During Red River's productive years, about 100 miles of track were in service.

Logging trucks, Caterpillar tractors, and chain saws came next. Approximately 200 million board feet a year were cut, 60 to 70 percent of the trees being cut in Plumas County. The Paul Bunyan trademark of Red River Lumber Company accurately portrayed the powerful role played by the company.

In 1945, with a diminished timber resource, Red River sold to Fruit Growers Supply for $3.5 million. Collins Pine purchased the electric railroad line running from Chester to Red River Junction, the latter name being changed to Clear Creek. Fruit Growers' Supply sold out a decade later, auctioning off the company town houses to individual buyers. Red River became a memory.

The Towle brothers from Sacramento utilized motorized log trucks after having successfully used a steam tractor at Slate Creek in 1912. In 1913, logs were hauled by trucks from the landing to their sawmill about a mile from the Quincy-Meadow Valley Road. By mid-summer of 1913, Towle's trucks were making six to eight trips daily, carrying 3,000 board feet of lumber to the Quincy Western Railway, 4 miles away. From there, it went by train to the company factory in Sacramento.

Graeagle Lumber Company also saw the advantage of trucks. Their holdings and contracts were for about 400 million board feet of timber in 1920, but it was scattered in checkerboard fashion in practically every direction from their mill, the largest single unit having 150 million feet. Logging roads were constructed at a cost of about $1,250 per mile. Four 7.5-ton trucks, equipped with 8.5-ton utility trailers, as well as another four 4.5-ton trucks, were put to work, allowing their single band sawmill to cut an average of 70,000 board feet per ten-hour day, or 13 million board feet annually.

By the 1930s, only a half dozen Plumas operators still used railroads, most supplemented by trucks. Ford, GMC, and Dodge Grahams were taking over from the railroads. By the end of World War II, only Quincy Lumber Company (until 1955) and Clover Valley Lumber (until 1957) still ran logging railroads.

Crawler tractors, known as Caterpillars or "Cats," revolutionized logging. The two largest Cat competitors, Best Tractor Company and Holt Tractor Company, merged in 1925 to form Allis-Chalmers and the tractor age was underway.

In 1921, Red River purchased a 55-horsepower Holt tractor. The next year, they acquired three new 65-horsepower Caterpillars. By 1925, a fleet of 16 Caterpillar tractors was operating at Camp 33. Graeagle Lumber Company acquired its first tractor in 1925 and Spanish Peak Lumber Company had replaced its donkeys with tractors by 1927.

By the mid-1920s, Nibley-Stoddard Lumber Company introduced the first Cat to the Cromberg woods. However, the operator had not mastered the machine and ran it into the millpond. Nibley-Stoddard of Santa Cruz had arrived in Cromberg in 1923 where they built a sawmill on what today is called the Old Mill Pond Road, opposite Mt. Tomba. That same year, they also constructed a 1.25-mile railroad incline up the steep mountain, a 35 to 69 percent grade. A large steam donkey was placed at the top of the rail line with a 1.625-inch steel cable. A Shay engine hauled empty flatcars along tracks into the woods and returned to the top of the incline loaded. The loaded cars were then lowered down the incline to the mill, unloaded, and pulled back up to be reconnected to the Shay and make the trip again. The Nibley-Stoddard Mill burned in 1926 and was never rebuilt. The cement foundations from the incline bridge across the old highway can be seen across the street from Mt. Tomba's front door.

Chainsaws were the next step in logging technology. In 1905, the first gasoline-powered chainsaw was used, but it was not portable. The 1918 Pitman saw weighed 210 pounds and was mounted on a 4.5-by-6-foot frame. Its power was furnished by a two-cylinder, two cycle gasoline motor that developed 6 horsepower. California's Dow Pump and Engine Company produced a rugged, powerful chainsaw in 1923 that required wheel mounting, thus limiting its usage, but it was able to fall and buck 70,000 board feet daily by the mid-1930s. Red River used 50-pound electric chainsaws for five or six years for falling and bucking. Their power was generated by a Cat's engine, but the constant need to move the chainsaw at the cutting location required constant movement of the Cat and painstaking care in moving the electric cord.

Plumas County lumberman Art West introduced Dow Pump and Engine Company gasoline powered falling saws in 1934 to loggers at Delleker, Clover Valley, and Graeagle. For four or five years, these chainsaws were well received until the introduction of two-man Titans, Mercurys, and Malls shortly after the end of World War II. Among this line up of saws were the 185-pound Distons, Canadian IELs weighing a little over 100 pounds, and the 145-pound Titans. Almost immediately after their debut, single-user saws came into use.

Collins Pine came to Chester in 1941 and began what has been for more than six decades the largest family owned lumbering operation in Plumas County. Approximately 90,000 acres of Plumas and Tehama County timberland are owned by the Collins family, almost 50,000 of it in Plumas County. Collins Pine sawmill is the second most productive in Plumas County.

The International truck in front is loaded with the second log (8,360 board feet) of a pine tree cut at Grizzly Forebay. The White truck in back holds the third log (7,220 board feet). Left to right is Ben Pauly, Bus Egbert, Chris Egbert, and Bob Lowrey II. The trucks were in the Plumas County Fair parade, August 1949.

Truman D. Collins and his son Everell Stanton Collins obtained the first Collins lands in 1902. The Collins operation disdained the old "cut and run" practice of cutting all the best trees. Truman Collins II decided to use the sustained yield method of having as many new trees growing as those cut down each year. He developed a long-range master plan based on the theory that the same number of board feet could be cut each year in perpetuity.

A monstrous sawmill, duplexes for employee housing, a cook house, machine shop, and logging equipment shop were constructed, some of which are still visible from Highway 36. Logging roads were constructed and five trucks were delivering the logs to the Red River Railroad line in Chester. For nearly two years, Collins sold approximately 85 million board feet per year to Red River Lumber. Collins Pine sawmill began operations in March 1943, using a single band head rig that cut 8,000 to 10,000 board feet per hour. The first load of Collins Pine lumber was shipped from the mill in April 1943. The millpond held 10 million board feet of logs and 200 men were employed year round in the mill and woods.

Cheney California Lumber of Greenville was the successful high bidder for the first Plumas National Forest skyline timber sale in Plumas County in July 1968. The site of the 17.3 million board foot sale was 17 miles southeast of Greenville.

Skyline logging works on the same general principal as a ski lift. Two high points are located opposite each other and above the felled timber and a cable

The Quincy Lumber Company mill was established by F.S. Murphy Lumber Company on the present site of Plumas Pines Shopping Center. A millpond, railroad, houses for workers, and tepee slash burner were all located here.

Men with caulked boots called "corks" and a piked pole balanced on logs floating in the millpond. They moved the logs across the pond to the slip for transport into the mill for sawing. These "pond monkeys" were working the millpond at Quincy Lumber Company's mill. Ben Berry is on the left.

is stretched from one side of the canyon to the other between the two points. A radio-operated carriage with a long cable tail is moved along the top horizontal cable to a location above the logs in the canyon. From this point, the end of a dangling cable is lowered to the ground and logs attached to it. The load is then lifted and transported to a landing where it is loaded on trucks for the mill.

Helicopter logging was inaugurated in Plumas County in 1971. The U.S. Forest Service selected Lights Creek Canyon as the location for the nation's first helicopter timber sale. Lights Creek Canyon was a maze of abrupt slopes. Erosion was a serious concern and preservation of its picturesque quality was desired.

Plumas Lumber Company of Crescent Mills, with Jack Erickson as president, won the helicopter timber sale bid in January 1971. Sikorsky S-61A helicopters with a lifting capacity of 8,000 pounds were contracted from Columbia Construction Helicopters of Portland, Oregon. After that, airborne harvests ranged from 39,376,000 board feet at Happy Valley to 110 million board feet at the Baloney cut over the next 15 years. Although helicopters create a minimum of disturbance, their high operating costs limit their practical application.

The lumber business has been Plumas County's leading industry since it replaced gold at the beginning of the twentieth century.

But now, due to national forest policy changes, environmental pressure, and a shifting economy, only two companies operate sawmills in Plumas County: Sierra Pacific Industries (old Meadow Valley Mill) in Quincy and Collins Pine in

Chester. Other reasons for mill closures include automation. Whereas a typical sawmill cutting 100,000 feet per shift in the 1940s through the 1970s required 25 men per eight-hour shift, in the 1990s, 15 men were all that were required. Sierra Pacific and Collins Pine each make a greater use of their by-products today. Bark, chips, and sawdust are all used. Old-time teepee burners have been replaced by sawdust-fueled power plants.

Plumas County's timberlands show the marks of over a half-century of unregulated logging followed by another three-quarters of a century of increased, intense regulated logging. Timber production is at an all-time low as Plumas County seeks to channel its economy to tourism. However, it is still a beautiful, renewable natural resource, providing jobs for local residents, as well as a place of pleasure for hikers, campers, fisherman, and hunters.

Part of the sawmilling process was to move the cut green lumber to a grading and storage area. This photo shows new lumber on the "green chain" at Collins Pine Lumber Mill in Chester c. 1948.

7. HYDROELECTRIC POWER: THE FEATHER RIVER CANYON AND THE "STAIRWAY OF POWER"

Six of Plumas County's eight major hydropower plants are located on the North Fork of the Feather River. Lake Almanor and Bucks Lake provide the largest share of water for hydropower from reservoirs.

In 1879, California's first hydroelectric power site was developed, although power installations could not take place until the 1880 invention of the Pelton waterwheel. Pelton's wheel was recognized as a "major breakthrough in the efficient utilization of falling water as an energy source." The first hydropower Pelton wheel installation in California was at Highgrove, near Colton in southern California, and Nevada City–Grass Valley in northern California in 1887.

Two years later, the Quincy Electric Light and Power Company was formed in 1889. A 300-foot-long reservoir was constructed to collect water from Gansner Creek, and by 1917 Quincy Electric Light and Power was delivering service to 160 homes and businesses. The 32-foot-by-38-foot concrete block powerhouse is still standing on the Bucks Lake Road.

Hydroelectric power introduced itself to the Feather River Canyon in 1908, during the same years as the WPRR construction. Big Bend Powerhouse, the first powerhouse, now under Lake Oroville, was built by the Eureka Power Company. In order to maintain a constant flow for the powerhouse, it was recognized that some kind of water control would be needed.

Julius M. Howells, a civil engineer, saw the potential for a storage reservoir in Big Meadows. He envisioned a huge lake in the 50-square-mile valley, fed by a drainage area of nearly 500 square miles. Howells presented his reservoir plan to publisher Edwin Earl, a newspaper magnate and citrus fruit shipper. Earl was interested, as was his brother Guy Earl of Oakland. Arthur Breed, Oakland's city auditor and a prominent real estate agent, was also impressed. The trio immediately began to develop a plan to acquire the valley and build their dam.

With a satchel of cash and a suave business approach, Breed contacted Big Meadows ranch owners to purchase options on their property. To those who questioned him, he merely stated he planned to resell the optioned land. Greenville resident Augustus Bidwell assisted Breed. On April 3, 1902, the *Plumas National Bulletin* reported that Breed had purchased Butt Valley in its entirety; "It is surmised that the lands will go to a cattle syndicate." Bidwell took credit for successfully handling the large transaction, while Breed continued his Big Meadows pursuit.

Breed, Bidwell, and Howells began to suspect Greenville's G.P. Cornell of having similar, secret plans for developing a Big Meadows storage reservoir. With the gold miners' doctrine "prior in time, prior in right" still recognized as the water law in the west, Howells and Bidwell trekked down the North Fork of the Feather River. About 2 miles downstream, they came upon two men who had been sent by Cornell. The men were nailing their own notice of water appropriation on a tree next to the river.

Believing these two were next bound for the county courthouse in Quincy, Howells and Bidwell acted quickly. Upon reaching Big Meadows, their first move was to cut the telephone line leading to Quincy, preventing the offending twosome from calling the county recorder to arrange for an evening meeting. Bidwell sped to Quincy, located the county recorder, and filed his papers at 8:25 p.m., April 8, 1902. Cornell's men arrived to do the same at 9:15 p.m. Howells and Bidwell had won the water appropriation battle by 50 minutes. The local newspaper reported, "Our citizens should feel rejoiced at the prosperous future which this enterprise and others related to it bring into view."

With their cards now on the table, the Earl brothers began seeking financial backing for their huge enterprise. The Western Power Company was soon created and 50,000 shares of capital stock issued for $5 million.

Action to condemn resistant dairy ranches began in May 1902 and continued throughout the onset of construction in 1911. Suits were initiated against approximately 40 Big Meadows property owners over the years. The company wanted it all. Because of the monumental scope and expense of their project, the Earl brothers invited eastern capitalists to inspect Big Meadows in June 1906. New York and Boston financiers were favorably impressed, as was multimillionaire Clarence Mackay, son of Virginia City Comstock multi-multimillionaire John Mackay. With solvency assured by the new brigade of corporate owners, the company changed its name to Great Western Power Company in 1906. The name was again changed in 1915 to Great Western Power Company of California, a name it retained until its sale to Pacific Gas and Electric Company (PG&E) in 1930.

Water rights for the North Fork of the Feather River were now consolidated under Great Western's control with the purchases of Cornell's Gold State Power, the Eureka Power Company, and Big Meadows, the linch pin in the North Fork hydro master plan. One roadblock remained before construction could begin: Prattville. This was a stable community of 75 to 100 residents, many homes, several large stores, and two hotels. They were pleased with the site of their settlement and saw no reason to sell.

Power company officials were stymied. Battles with individual ranchers were one thing, but a whole town was another. Buying out each and every homeowner and businessman would be expensive and time consuming, yet there seemed to be no alternative—until July 4, 1910. No one has proven whether it was arson or a timely coincidence. The entire Prattville population was enjoying a holiday picnic and baseball game a few miles from town when suddenly they heard a huge explosion. Looking toward town, they saw a rising pillar of smoke and flame. Most of the town was burned to the ground in a matter of hours. Was it arson or just an unfortunate accident? Prattville citizens did not think it was the latter. Whatever the cause, by 1912, Great Western Power had title to the land.

To build the massive Lake Almanor dam, people, tools, supplies, food, and tons of aggregate for cement were needed. A one-lane, rough roadway was hacked through the woods in 1910 from Greenville to the Nevis Tavern and dam site near today's Canyon Dam.

Six- and eight-mule teams did the hauling at first—three days for a round trip from Keddie. Then, as the automotive age began, truck fleets were contracted. The 52-mile round trip could then be accomplished in ten hours. Local freight haulers were upset. The trucks created a sea of dust and frightened mules and horses. Petitions circulated demanding a county ordinance to limit the modern "monsters" to night hours only, but the locals lost.

Horace Bucklin's land, including the site of the Bucks Ranch Hotel, was inundated by the waters of Bucks Lake when the reservoir was completed in 1928.

In addition to supplies and labor, power was needed. Despite the wild, remote lay of the land along Butt Creek, the company built a small hydroelectric plant there that transmitted power to the Big Meadows dam site. They also completed a small dam at the mouth of Butt Valley in 1913 that was enlarged in 1924, then again in 1996.

Engineer Julius Howells drew a plan based on Eastwood's multiple arch design, having a series of 22 huge arches made of steel and aggregate. Completion of the multi-arch structure would make Big Meadows the largest storage reservoir in North America at the time and the second largest in the world, with only the gigantic Assounan Dam in Egypt surpassing it.

T.B. Walker's Red River Lumber Company moved in on Big Meadows, falling the stately groves of sugar pine and fir. Over the next two years, 300 million board feet of merchantable timber was removed.

The 60-man dam construction crew built a rustic camp, now called Canyon Dam. Cottages were erected for a dozen families and bunkhouses for the 50 single men. Each cottage had running water, a bath, toilet, and eventually electricity. The work crew also built warehouses and a rock crushing plant, installed an aerial tram, and erected a sawmill before actual work began on the dam. A small eight-bed hospital was built, run by Dr. Fred Davis, who was paid $1 per month by each employee. During the dam construction period (1910–1914), Dr. Davis stated the men had their "share of serious accidents, but no epidemics."

The Belden Powerhouse penstock is 1,292 feet long with a drop of 770 feet. The powerhouse, completed in 1969, takes water from Belden Forebay below Seneca on the North Fork Feather River.

By mid-October 1912, 20,000 cubic yards of cement had been poured and five of the 22 arches and 40 percent of the structure was finished. More than $500,000 had been expended in that year alone.

Unfortunately, bedrock leaks and other problems occurred. In March 1913, the state-appointed railroad commission ordered work stopped. Commission investigations found the bedrock base to be nothing more than a layer of crumbly lava material, insufficient to support the immense structure. They said that it should be torn down and restarted from scratch at a different site, which was discouraging for company officials, but the setback was for the best. Howells was sent back to the drawing board.

Within a couple of weeks, the new plans were drawn up and approved. By mid-May, work was progressing rapidly on the new foundation. The old arches were dynamited over and used as fill for the new dam. By mid-September, the diversion tunnel was finished and the water was now directed into the tunnel so actual dam construction could begin. A massive concrete core was constructed while 2,400 cubic yards of earth was dumped in the fill site daily. To obtain the necessary fill, hydraulic monitors were used to obtain dirt and boulders. The growing pile of dirt surrounding the concrete core gradually grew into a 72-foot-high bulwark of earth. It consisted of over 250,000 cubic yards of fill.

In February 1914, the massive Big Meadows earth-fill dam and concrete spillway was finished. By mid-March, 19 feet of water stood between the dam site and Meadow View Hotel; a month later, the Big Springs section was entirely flooded. Water was backed up to the main street of old Prattville. The white cemetery and the three Big Meadows Native American cemeteries had supposedly been moved above the anticipated water level.

In July, Great Western Power Company president Mortimer Fleishacker visited the reservoir and proclaimed the endeavor an "epoch-making event." He also announced the official name "Almanor," named by Guy Earl, for his three daughters Alice, Martha, and Elinor. It took four years for Lake Almanor to fill to capacity. Magnificent Big Meadows was now a reservoir of nearly 40 square miles, 13 miles long and 6 miles wide. Its holding capacity was 220,000 acre-feet of water.

Hydropower demands were increasing, so a new and higher dam was built between 1925 and 1927, quadrupling water storage capacity. The new dam was built directly to the side and below the old one, rising 130 feet above the North Fork's streambed. The combination of the new and old dam now amounted to 1,389,300 cubic yards of fill. Lake Almanor's storage capacity quadrupled. Further expansion in the early 1950s enlarged the lake to 47 square miles, extending to the very edge of Chester. Water storage capacity was increased to its present 1.3 million acre-feet.

Red River Lumber Company built Plumas County's second hydropower plant on Hamilton Branch to escape paying Great Western Power and to provide electricity for the lumber mill and town of Westwood. Water was supplied by diverting Hamilton Branch into ditches and pipes to the powerhouse. Walker

Lake, known now as Mountain Meadows Reservoir, was completed in 1924 to guarantee year-round water for the hydro plant. PG&E purchased the powerhouse in 1945 and extensively renovated it.

Caribou Powerhouse was the second hydro plant built by Great Western (Butt Valley was first), becoming part of the Feather River's "Stairway of Power." Work on the immense Caribou hydropower project would take place during three calendar years, 1919 through 1921, but only 22 months in all because of its remoteness.

A constant flow was necessary for proper hydro plant operations. The rushing waters of the North Fork could slow to a trickle in August or September during low snowpack years. To insure a reliable water supply, Great Western decided to build an 11,200-foot tunnel through the mountain ridge near the old Prattville Hotel to carry water from Lake Almanor to the Butt Valley side of the mountain. Upon completion of the tunnel, the Lake Almanor water would drop into Butt Creek and then flow 6 miles in that stream. A small impounding dam was located near that creek's junction with the North Fork. From there, water would again be diverted into 9,200-foot Tunnel No. 2, coming out more than 1,000 feet above the powerhouse.

Each of the 12 camps Great Western erected had dwellings and bunkhouses, complete with spring cots and wood stoves, hot showers, and sanitation facilities. Some even had lawns and gardens. Each camp had a commissary and a well-equipped clubhouse, including moving pictures. Each had a first-aid ward, while Camp No. 5 was the main hospital site. The hospital had two wards and was equipped with operating table, modern dressing room, x-ray outfit, and all the requisites for medical and surgical attention. Each employee paid $1 per month for medical coverage and $1.25 per day for room and board. Great Western laborers worked ten hours a day for $6. Tunnel men worked eight hours for $7.25, while carpenters received $7.60 for their eight-hour day.

By December 1920, a little over 1 million pounds of fresh beef, 900,000 pounds of potatoes, 57,000 dozen eggs, and 26,000 gallons of canned fruits and vegetables were delivered to the project. Overall, worker numbers varied from 800 to 1,900 men on the job at a time.

Meanwhile, at the Belden, or south end of the project, teams were hauling supplies from the WPRR over a hastily graded road. Provisions were unloaded at Listo, then moved across the river to Howell's at the junction of the East Branch and North Fork. To expedite the project, contractors Stone & Webster built a 9-mile standard-gauge railroad from Listo to Caribou and the powerhouse in 1919.

The mountainous region between Caribou and Butt Valley was the most isolated and rugged section. Machinery, tools, dynamite, food, beds, clothes, and hay and grain had to be packed by mules on trails to the construction camps. From Caribou, a tramway was built on the steep mountainside behind the power plant to the Oak Flat area. Freight was sent up it to a narrow gauge rail line, then to two more tramways to connect with two additional narrow gauge lines, each set of tracks being at a different elevation.

The Caribou Powerhouse was completed by May 1921. The powerhouse was 175 feet long, 100 feet wide, and 125 feet high. To guarantee year-round water delivery to the Caribou Powerhouse, Great Western decided to convert another peaceful mountain valley into a man-made lake; thus, Butt Valley became Butt Lake in 1924. The remaining hotel in the old town of Butt Valley was burned and everything else, including a small steam engine used in construction of the dam, was inundated. Reservoir capacity of the new lake was 49,929 acre-feet.

Building contractors R.C. Storrie and Robert Muir saw Great Western's success and developed a man-made lake idea of their own. They envisioned Bucks Ranch becoming Bucks Lake. Soon, they formed the Feather River Power Company and purchased the 1,000 plus acre Bucks Ranch and adjacent properties. They embarked on the project in early 1926 and the three-year, $8 million project was finished in late 1928. Due to financial problems, however, the Feather River Power Company was forced to sell out to Great Western Power Company, who completed the project.

Bucks Lake was the primary storage reservoir, with two pipes running directly under the new dam into Bucks Creek, guiding the water to Lower Bucks Diversion Dam. From this smaller dam, the water would flow in a 54-inch pipe through a 5,650-foot tunnel to Grizzly Creek. Water would then flow down Grizzly Creek to Grizzly Forebay. From Grizzly Forebay, the water would flow into a 9,000-foot tunnel, much of it through solid rock, and then to the head of the

Lake Almanor was created when the dam near Canyon Dam was finished in 1914. Inundating beautiful Big Meadows, once home to Maidu Indians, cattle and dairy ranches, and a number of resorts, it is now a water sports recreation favorite.

103

penstocks. The 4,800-foot-long penstocks would deliver the water directly into the Bucks Powerhouse situated on the North Fork Feather River. No housing was handy within miles of the powerhouse site, so a construction camp opposite the powerhouse was blasted out of the canyon side and named after R.C. Storrie, the originator of the Bucks Lake hydro project.

A tramway was constructed from the powerhouse on the river to the top of the ridge bordering the canyon. From that point to Bucks Ranch, a distance of approximately 8 miles, a narrow gauge railroad was built. These were used for the transportation of men and supplies to the Bucks Lake dam.

In 1928, the powerhouse and penstocks were completed, the main earth dam at Bucks Lake soon thereafter. At completion, the rock-filled dam was 118 feet high and 1,220 feet long. Bucks Lake itself covered 1,827 surface acres and contained 101,926 acre-feet of water storage capacity. It took seven years to completely fill.

To the northwest, Three Lakes was developed and tapped by a pipeline to Lower Bucks Lake. During that 8-mile stretch, the waters of 21 smaller creeks were collected and added to the flow. PG&E, purchasers of Great Western Power Company in 1930, allocated several hundred million dollars for an additional six hydroelectric powerhouses and four new dams on the Feather River. In addition, 26.5 miles of tunnels were driven through solid rock to facilitate the projects.

The Rock Creek and Cresta powerhouses and dams were the first ones built in 1947 to 1950. Construction of Rock Creek Powerhouse began at the same time as the dam, located almost 8 miles above the powerhouse. From the dam, a portion of the water is diverted into a tunnel 6.5 miles long and 25 feet in diameter to the powerhouse. Total cost for the Rock Creek Powerhouse and dam was $35.4 million. Cresta Dam, 113 feet high and 384 feet wide, diverted water into 4 miles of tunnel 26 feet in diameter. From the tunnel, huge pipes conveyed the water into the Cresta Powerhouse. The Cresta Powerhouse and dam, also built between 1947 and 1950, cost $26.5 million.

Stage two in PG&E's "Stairway of Power" development took place from 1955 to 1958, with three new powerhouses completed: Butt Valley, Caribou No. 2, and Poe. Caribou Powerhouse No. 2 operations were similar to No. 1's. Water from Butt Valley Reservoir ran through a 1.5-mile-long tunnel, 13 feet in diameter, to a 10.5-foot diameter penstock nearly half a mile long. This dropped down a 60-degree slope into the powerhouse. To cut the trench for this penstock, bulldozers had to be anchored at the end of stout cables from other bulldozers above. Eleven years later, the Belden Powerhouse was completed in 1969, thus ending PG&E's postwar projects.

The Feather River Canyon is a geologic marvel whose history is highlighted by the Maidu, gold miners, railroading, hydroelectric power development, and highway construction. The Feather River was named by Spanish explorers as "El Rio de las Plumas," or River of Feathers, supposedly for the large numbers of waterfowl who made it their seasonal home. The North Fork's headwaters are above Lake Almanor and Quincy, while its Middle Fork originates in Sierra Valley. The smaller South Fork heads out of Little Grass Valley and Pilot Peak.

The Caribou Powerhouse was completed in 1921 under great difficulty. A number of tramways, a railroad, and several pack trails all had to be built to ship supplies to this remote site along the North Fork Feather River between Belden and Lake Almanor.

The Maidu traditionally lived and hunted along the branches of the Feather River, particularly in the areas of Pulga, Camp Rodgers, Belden, Twain, and Keddie. About 1900, Susan, a Maidu born on Yellow Creek near Belden, married Bob Belden, a white miner. They filed a homestead on today's Belden and received legal title to the land. Belden opened a saloon and general store during the railroad construction years and erected a dozen cabins for travelers and year-round residents. The Belden post office opened in 1909 and a three-story hotel, the Riverside, was built.

Twain had its beginnings as Kingsbury's Ferry, the site of a privately owned river crossing business. Over the years, it was a supply spot for canyon miners. In 1905, it was selected as a railroad construction camp. Nearby Gray's Flat was an early mining camp turned sawmill operation and receiving end for the Spanish Peak Mill tramway.

In 1912, WPRR inaugurated the "Fishermen's Special." They carried anglers by train from the Bay Area, Sacramento, and locations along the line to the North Fork for fishing. The train arrived at daybreak; fishermen got off at any mile post they wanted, fished all day, and reboarded to go home in the early evening. Tobin resort was built in 1915, catering to the Fishermen's Special.

Moseley & Grenke established a grocery store at Tobin, and soon a billiard parlor, barbershop, and movie theater were erected. The present tavern was built in 1937, 20 rental cabins and 2 sleeping dormitories were erected in 1947, 52 trailer units were scattered among the trees, and during the 1948 to 1950 period, the Tobin Bar employed six bartenders. In one three-month period, more than

700 cases of hard liquor were sold. Tobin's liquor account was said to be the largest in northern California. Indian Jim School was built in the 1950s and named for James Lee, a Maidu who lived and gardened along the river with his family of five.

Camp Rodgers developed as a summer resort with a hotel and guest cabins above the railroad tracks. The resort remained popular until the early 1930s, but closed with the decline of railroad passenger business and completion of the Feather River Canyon highway in 1937. PG&E took it over as a work site in 1962.

Soda Bar, on the original Indian Valley trail, was the site of gold mining activity, as well as a ferry, store, and small community. Across the river was Iron Bar, where in 1916 Paxton was founded when the IVRR built a connection with WPRR. The hotel built by IVRR and WPRR was named after Elmer Paxton, one of Engels Mine's executives.

Monumental in Feather River Canyon's historic accomplishments was the construction of the Feather River Canyon Highway. Construction required three tunnels, twelve bridges, and nine years to build.

The Feather River Canyon was indeed a busy place during the post–World War II years. The Hitching Post, Jack's Place, Feather River Hot Springs, Virgilia Hotel and Café, and a number of others were built as restaurants and saloons to satisfy hunger and refreshment needs of canyon workers and residents. The Canyon is quieter now, but the residents there maintain a sense of community among themselves and reflect upon the "good old days."

Massive turbines in the Bucks Creek Powerhouse are pummeled with water traveling more than 200 miles per hour.

8. Big Meadows: Chester and Lake Almanor

Big Meadows was a breathtaking, scenic high-elevation meadow that stretched approximately 20 miles in length and 3 in width. The vast green meadow contained islands of magnificent sugar and ponderosa pine. Before it was made a lake, the gorgeous basin teemed with sweet ferns and wildflowers of all kinds and colors, including tiger lilies, white lilies, and honeysuckle. The *Plumas National Bulletin* proclaimed the following on June 29, 1889:

> If anyone wants to spend a few weeks, where he can breathe pure air, drink the finest mountain spring water, catch all the fish he wants . . . up to six pounds . . . shoot deer . . . and have his eyes continually feasting on the most picturesque and beautiful scenery in the world, come to Big Meadows.

S.A.D. Puter described the Big Meadows area before 1910 in *Looters of the Public Domain*: "unquestionably the finest body of Sugar Pine timber in the world existed in the basin known as the Big Meadows of Plumas County."

Winding through the meadow was the North Fork of the Feather River. Stream flow was mostly at a peaceful glide with alternately swift, turbulent sections. Many of the quietly flowing stretches supported bulrushes and pond lilies, bordered by lush grasslands and intersected by scores of different sized tributaries. By the 1870s, cattlemen and dairymen's farmhouses dotted the valley and meadow edges along with their dairy and hay barns. Herds of cattle grazed the lush meadows. Sportsmen fished for trout, and hunted ducks and Canada geese.

The first known white men to pass through the valley were '49ers on their way to the mining regions, traveling by way of Lassen's Trail in the late summer and early fall of 1849. Lassen's Trail, coming south from Pit River, entered Big Meadows near Hamilton Branch, proceeded southwest through the meadows, and on to Deer Creek and the Sacramento Valley.

Of the approximately 8,000 '49ers who used Lassen's Trail, J. Goldsborough Bruff and William Swain kept the most detailed accounts known today. Swain described Big Meadows in his late October 1849 crossing as "very swampy, covered with heavy grass, surrounded by a heavy belt of timber, and on the east and south are mountains reaching up into the regions of everlasting snow."

From 200 to 600 Maidu lived in the foothills surrounding the valley when the '49ers passed through. Parties of Gold Lake seekers passed through Big Meadows in 1850, followed by more and more prospectors in the ensuing years. The disruption of the way of life of the Native Americans was clearly underway.

The Big Meadows area had no gold, but nearby Seneca and Caribou on the North Fork of the Feather River did. During the same period, the number of Sacramento Valley cattle ranchers and their stock increased in numbers. Cattlemen were looking for green summer grasses for pasturage, as well as relief from the valley's scorching summer heat.

By 1854, the numbers of cattle, miners, and other travelers coming to the area were sufficient to encourage Samuel Knight and Ned St. Felix to capitalize on this traffic, and in that year they built a toll bridge across the North Fork of the Feather River in Big Meadows.

By the end of the decade, a number of Sacramento Valley cattle ranchers had also begun making summer cattle drives to Humbug Valley and Butt Valley. William Bunnell was one of those situated at Butt Valley. Nearby Humbug Valley activity had increased to the point that a sawmill was erected and a hotel was built in 1858. Among the Big Meadows cattle ranchers by the late 1850s were John Bidwell, James Lee, J. Benner, George Freeman, Henry Landt, Reuben Stover, and six or eight more.

James Walleck established the first sawmill in Big Meadows in 1858. Battista Baccala and Charles Dotta settled in 1870. In 1872, Charles Dotta's brother Floriana purchased the valley's first permanent settler's ranch, that of Joshua Abbot. Jonathan Martin settled on 160 acres in 1873. During the three-decade period of the 1860s through 1880s, other settlers were Dr. Willard Pratt (Prattville), John Hamilton (Hamilton Branch) and Burt Johnson, as well as the Baccala brothers Battista, Victor, and Guiseppi (the latter anglicized to Joseph or Joe), the Becrafts, the Baileys, the Butterfields, and the Holmes.

Peter Olsen was born in 1824 in Norway and immigrated to the United States in 1842. He came overland to California in 1852, and following a disappointing trip to the Fraser River gold rush in Canada in 1858, committed the rest of his life to cattle ranching.

Because Sacramento Valley's green grasses were changing to brown by June each year, in the late 1850s and early 1860s, Olsen rounded up his cattle and drove them to the mountains for summer grazing; in the fall, he drove them back to their home ranch in the Chico area. Olsen preempted 160 acres of land in what is now southeastern Chester.

Jeremiah and Melissa Bailey had settled in Big Meadows in 1859. By 1867, Melissa had three children: Gus, Frank, and Alice. Melissa Bailey epitomized the courageous contributions of the county's frontier women. Jeremiah contracted pneumonia and died in 1867. Melissa was a woman of strength, a determined,

Big Meadows was a popular resort area for Sacramento Valley tourists from the 1860s until the creation of Lake Almanor. Its cool waters provided spectacular trout fishing and waterfowl hunting, while its tranquil setting provided relaxation from the stress of urban life.

brave lady. She purchased 160 acres of Big Meadows land and established a ranch for her family. She was instrumental in the construction of the valley's first one-room log school building on her ranch in 1868, known as the Melissa School. She later married Peter Olsen and had three more children, all boys.

Reuben and Thaddeus Stover came to Big Meadows in 1859 or 1860 by packhorse from the Sacramento Valley with Peter Olsen. The Stovers preempted 160 acres each, and when the Homestead Act was passed in 1862 they were each able to obtain 160 acres more on which to build their homes. Soon they had about 700 acres and were the largest property owners in the basin.

As the years passed, their stock increased in numbers. Soon they were in the dairy business, with three men hand-milking 60 cows a day. Hand churns were used for making butter until water-powered churns were developed a decade or two later. The butter was packed in firkins and shipped in wagons over the Humboldt Road to Chico. On the home trip, they would bring back staples, clothing, groceries, and peanuts and mixed hard candy for the kids' treats on Sundays and holidays.

Jacob and Elizabeth Benner moved to Big Meadows in 1867, having pastured their cattle there for years during the summer and fall. Their ranch was located near the creek that still bears the family name, Benner Creek.

Permanent settlers weren't the only ones coming to Big Meadows during the second half of the 1860s. Sacramento Valley residents began coming to the area to escape the valley's hot summers and to find recreation, hunting, and fishing. Dr.

Willard Pratt responded to their needs in 1867. On an elevated spot next to the river, he bought out the only log cabin owner in the area and built his home-hotel. The well-built establishment quickly caught on and became a popular resort.

A businessman as well as a medical doctor, Pratt's hotel became a major stage stop along the Chico-Honey Lake Road. Next, he laid out a town site, and by 1868 three new structures were erected and operating: M.B. Abbot's general store, a saloon with billiard table, and a post office. Two years later, Prattville was described as a "small village," consisting of Pratt's hotel, Abbot's store, Charley Mullen's blacksmith shop, a saloon, shoe shop, and "five or six other houses, some of which contain families."

Picking up on Big Meadows' growth, the county newspaper reported, "the Meadows are fast filling with those families who wintered their stock in the Sacramento Valley, and some who have not lived here before."

One of the tourists who was a great lover of flowers had additional praise: "I have been botanizing in the western arm of Big Meadows since the spring of 1860, and I must say I have not found a greater variety of flowers and plants in any other part of this state from San Diego to this point."

Temporarily interrupting the scenic beauty was a destructive fire that burned Pratt's Hotel to the ground in 1876. Undaunted, he rebuilt an even more impressive hotel the next year. The two-story structure was comprised of 26 sleeping rooms, stately parlors, and family lounges. Boating, fishing, hunting, and picturesque drives, including occasional picnic and camping trips to Mt. Lassen, were all offered to the guests along with the Big Meadows' delightful summer climate.

The nearby area around Pratt's Hotel grew. By 1880, there was a wagon shop, blacksmith shop, saloon, three general merchandise stores, numerous dwellings, and a population of around 100 people. The population of Seneca Township, which included Big Meadows and the North Fork of the Feather River, was 312 whites, 137 Native Americans, and 86 Chinese.

Prattville was not the only resort, though. At the upper end of Big Meadows, along the Red Bluff Road, Charles Littlefield and Burt Johnson each ran active hotels and saloons by the late 1870s. At the lower end of the meadows were Bidwell's Meadow View Hotel and the Nevis Tavern. Butterfield's was another smaller hotel on the North Fork about mid-way between Pratt's and Bunnell's. At the foot of today's Lake Almanor Peninsula, L. Wellington Bunnell built his fine hotel to compete with Dr. Pratt's.

Moving from Butt Valley, where he was a cattle rancher and had a general merchandise store, Bunnell settled in Big Meadows in 1868. The next year, he married pioneer widow Julia Lee and together they opened a popular summer resort. Bunnell's home-hotel was described in 1881 as "one of the finest to be found in the mountains . . . large and well furnished." Mrs. Bunnell cooked the meals, which were said to "challenge the appetites of the most ravenous tourist."

Then disaster hit in 1899 when fire destroyed it. Two years later, Bunnell built a new, plush three-story hotel with a carriage entrance and a long bridge across the river. It was normally filled to capacity with vacationers from as far away as San Francisco, and often they were forced to turn people away. The new hotel was a T-shaped structure with a breathtaking sunset view of Mt. Lassen. It had all the appropriate appurtenances—a boathouse, butcher shop, dairy barn and cellar, livestock, and poultry—but there was no liquor served, Bunnell preferring "family" guests.

In 1894, a post office was established at dairy rancher Burt Johnson's farmhouse-hotel. Now the five dairy ranching families—Peter Olsen, Reuben Stover, Thaddeus Stover, Oscar Martin, and Burwell "Burt" Johnson—living at the northern end of Big Meadows would have summer mail. Burt Johnson, a native of Chester, Missouri, and Oscar Martin, a native of Chester, Vermont, decided on the name of Chester for the post office.

A Presbyterian Church built in 1898 by John and Annie Bidwell on their summer home property about a mile out of the present town of Chester followed the post office. Services were held only in the summer when vacationing pastors came to preach. The post office and church were the only visible evidences of what was later to become the town of Chester.

After Burt Johnson died in 1907, the Chester post office was moved to the Olsen Ranch. As an improvement, Peter Olsen's son George built a small store, including an indoor post office, next to their ranch house for their cousin Maude Gay. Maude operated the store and became the second postmaster.

The Chester Post Office and Store was the one and only gathering spot for years in "downtown" Chester. These people are reflecting on the day's events in 1915.

Dairy rancher Oscar Martin subdivided a small part of his ranch on the north side of the Red Bluff–Susanville road into 37 lots in 1909. His daughter Edith Martin then subdivided 49 more lots in 1911. The same year, George, Nels, and Ed Olsen subdivided a small portion of their ranch on the south side of the Red Bluff–Susanville road into 116 lots, including a large school parcel. The lots were located south of today's Plumas Street, east and west from the Prattville Road to Melissa Avenue. The 200 or so lots placed for sale by Olsen and Martin became the nucleus of the town of Chester.

The earliest town library was started from Melissa Bailey-Olsen's collection of books placed in the Chester store and post office. The present Chester Library, built in 1929, still houses her collection. Melissa Bailey-Olsen's daughter Alice Bailey married Jonathan Martin's son Oscar. Alice had two children before dying at the age of 18. The Martin family donated the land for the Chester Library, courthouse, park, jail, fire hall, and elementary school. The Olsen-Martin legacy retains a memorable position in the history of Chester.

In 1914, Great Western Power began filling the Big Meadows with Lake Almanor's water, but Chester was still only a few dairy ranches, three or four houses, and the two Olsen stores. Except for the new lake and diminished grazing ground, life continued as usual for the Olsens, Martins, and Stovers. To accommodate vacationers deprived of the use of Pratt's Hotel, the Bunnell House,

A flat-bottomed steam-powered boat called the Meadowlark *skimmed along the lake portion of Big Meadows long before Great Western Power Company constructed Lake Almanor.*

and others, Nels Olsen built the Chester Hotel in 1914. Likewise, Reuben Stover began renting rooms in his 1862 ranch house, calling it the Hotel Stover.

As Olsen's Chester Hotel went up in 1914, so did Mt. Lassen—just 20 miles away! The volcanic mountain erupted numerous times, twice in June and three times in September. Charles Stover vividly remembered the ground rumbles felt at his ranch and the fiery explosion, which was visible from Chester, followed by big clouds of rolling smoke. When the alignment of those clouds and the wind zeroed directly in on Chester, ashes would sift down and if caught just right, "it would look like it was snowing on you."

Red River Lumber Company timber activity began changing things in the Chester area. A year-round logging camp known as Camp 57 was situated on today's Chester High School campus until 1937. It consisted of bunkhouses, cabins, a cookhouse, and lots of loggers. Red River property also included present-day home sites on First, Second, and Third Streets.

Red River Lumber Company headquarters was 12 miles away in Westwood, but its logging operations in Plumas County were the biggest in the county's history, trees being felled by the millions from 1912 to 1945. The introduction of loggers to Camp 57, plus the handful of dairy ranching families and summer vacationers quickly doubled the population of Chester. Chester was beginning to grow, not as a permanent town, but as a temporary logging suburb and an enjoyable, relaxing summer get-away.

For the quarter-century following the filling of Lake Almanor (1914–1940), Chester grew at a leisurely pace. There were enough people for Saturday night summer dances by 1918. The United States Forest Service ranger station tent was replaced by a regular building on Main Street in 1922. Post office boxes were installed the same year for the first time at the post office. Sixty-three customers signed up for the mail service; however, the post office itself was only open for business three days a week. The only winter mail came when Nels Olsen went to Prattville on horseback, sleigh, or skis when snow conditions permitted.

By 1926, Jack Wardlow had electric lights at his corner store–dance hall– apartments, the only electric lights in town. His power came from the plant in the old tank house. Edith Martin was selling more lots the same year on the old Red Bluff Road, now called Feather River Drive.

Charlie Stover and Earl McKenzie were running the Stover-McKenzie Cattle Company, which was becoming a big operation. They pastured their herd in Chester in summer and at Los Molinas in the winter, just as Peter Olsen, the Stovers, and the Baccala brothers had done during the last half of the previous century.

Stover and McKenzie started a rodeo for their ranch hands and local cowboys in 1920 in the fenced in area of the Stover Ranch at the edge of town. Cowboys, untamed range cattle, and unbroken horses provided exciting entertainment. Showing their daredevil makeup, girls participated in steer riding contests also. Prize money increased as professional cowboys began participating and attendance increased. A big beef barbecue was enjoyed when it was over. For two decades, the

Chester summer rodeo became the "Super Bowl" of northern Plumas County. By 1930, nearly 2,500 people enjoyed the rodeo and the small grandstands had to be enlarged. By 1937, they could seat 4,000 people, every seat being filled and another 1,000 standing up or sitting on top of their cars.

And though the rodeo itself required only a full late Sunday afternoon, the occasion began to include rodeo dances on both Saturday and Sunday evenings for $1 admission fee. Previewing Sunday afternoon's feature event, a parade began at noon with lots of horses, music, and a few floats. Pageant participants attired themselves in full cowboy regalia including chaps, red handkerchiefs tied about their necks, and six-shooters. However, all this fun proved to be too expensive for Stover and McKenzie. There was too much gambling and too many fights; every Saturday and Sunday evening dance had a number of brawls. Lasting from 9 p.m. to well past midnight, often nearly to dawn, the festive activity occurred at the large dance hall next to Wardlow's "Old Corner" store.

Dancing, drinking, and gaiety would go along smoothly for a while, but inevitably a quarrel between some logger and a cowboy would erupt into a wild, uncontrollable fight. For self-protection, everyone cleared out to the highway while the battle raged. Then they went back inside to dance until the next angry contest sent them scurrying to the highway again. These were predictable evenings of "dance, drink, fight—dance, drink, fight."

Eventually, some of the residents became more and more disgusted with "no law and no sheriff's deputies except the one or two sent during rodeo times." At the end of the 1938 barbecue, following a worse than usual drunken fight at the rodeo, Charlie Stover announced, "The hell with it; there won't be any more!" And there weren't; Chester rodeo days became history.

Little Reno, as Chester was locally known, was a wide-open town. Liquor, slot machines, blackjack, and craps were the busiest enterprises for owners of the Bear Club, Lassen Club, Eastside, Blue Fox, and Chester Club. The four or five "ladies of the night" at Romey's local bordello had plenty of business. Lumberjacks from the "dry" town of Westwood were steady customers during the evenings and weekends.

In 1931, the town consisted of Wardlow's Corner Grocery, a café, hotel, drugstore, butcher shop, four service stations, Denny Moore's Sport Shop, Maude Gay's grocery store and post office, ten rental cabins, and the aforementioned bars. Not until 1934 did the town have sufficient numbers to become an official voting precinct. Chester Elementary School, grades one through six, was the only school in town in 1930.

Jack and Ethel Thieler, annual summer vacationers to Chester from San Francisco, decided to make the mountains their home in 1930. Because Westwood was the only high school available for their son Al, Ethel went to Quincy to visit the Plumas County School District officials and county board of supervisors about the situation. She returned home with a $150 per month contract to become the first Plumas County school bus driver. Al fulfilled his parent's educational hopes for him, becoming a lawyer and county judge.

The Prattville Hotel in Big Meadows was built by Dr. Pratt in 1866 as a public house. It burned and was rebuilt in 1876, serving the public until 1910 when the construction of the Lake Almanor dam began. This view is of the rear of the hotel.

Electricity had arrived by the 1930s, although some had it as early as the mid-1920s. The power came from Red River Lumber Company's Camp 57. Home lighting was merely a dangling cord from the middle of the ceiling with a single light bulb.

Other than at Red River Lumber, there were less than a handful of telephones from the late 1920s to the early 1930s. Some enjoyed indoor water from their well and its electric pump, while others still had old-fashioned hand pumps in their kitchens. Outhouses were as common as indoor toilets during the 1930s. Clothes were washed in large tubs with water heated on the stove.

Clearly demonstrating the transition from old to new in the 1930s were the Rainbow Court Cottages built in Old Town Chester in 1930 by Jack and Ethel Thieler. They consisted of ten modern cottages, a restaurant, gas station, and automobile shop. The cottages were fully equipped housekeeping units with running water, electric heat, and electric ranges and ovens for cooking.

Walt Gasney, who had been a driver on the Red Bluff-to-Susanville stage, decided to "establish some roots" about the same time as the Thielers. Gasney constructed the Deer Horn Auto Court in Old Town that attracted many fishermen and hunters, who went with him to his hunting camp.

The biggest fire in the town's history occurred in 1934 at the three-story Lee Lodge on Main Street, owned by Minnie Lee West, burning the structure to the ground. A few other nearby buildings were also destroyed, the site of the fire being where today's Western Auto store and Elks Lodge are located.

Chester had no fire engine or fire department in the 1930s. The nearest help was a Deer Creek Meadows Civilian Conservation Corps Camp where a fire

The Chico-Prattville Stage ran every day except Sundays over the Humboldt Road. This photo shows the stage in 1905.

response vehicle was housed. Rushing over with its portable "billy pump," a backpack-type gas powered water pump, and hand tools, the Lee Lodge was ashes by the time the fire response vehicle arrived.

As a result of the fire's destruction, public concern for better fire protection soon led to contributions and the purchase of an old hand-pulled wagon with iron wheels. Later, additional contributions raised enough money to make the down payment on a new 1940 Ford firetruck, which arrived that same year. The new fire engine was housed in an old garage where the present fire station is located. When Chester residents were unable to raise enough contributions to make the first payment on the truck, the Chester Fire District was formed to retain ownership and taxes were levied. Joe Striplin became the fire chief from 1941 to 1974, not receiving a paycheck until the mid-1950s.

The 1934 fire was only half of Chester's destructive problems during the decade. A flood from the North Fork of the Feather River breached its banks, the 5- to 6-foot-deep water swiftly inundating Old Town Chester. Town inhabitants were forced to retreat to their rooftops where they remained until daylight before rescue crews could reach them. No one was lost, though one automobile was swept away and destroyed, and some 150 feet of the oil-surfaced Susanville–Red Bluff Highway was undermined and washed out.

Among those financially hurt by the flood were the half-dozen or so seasonal Chinese residents. Harry Kan, the most prominent man of the group, along with Leong Wong, Jack Ma, Frank Gee, and Wong Sing, lived in the Eastside Café on Main Street in Old Town. By the mid-1930s, Frank Gee moved out and purchased what is today the Mt. Lassen Club, operating it as a grocery store, restaurant, and gambling house.

The start of Collins Pine operations in 1941 inaugurated town stability and permanent growth. When Collins Pine opened with its bunkhouses, kitchen, and equipment sheds in 1941 and 1942, there were no stores west of the Feather River in "new town," only two houses, the dance hall, and six apartments known as the "Red Feather."

"Little Reno" days were ending. Charlie Stover and the repeal of prohibition had unintentionally started the change. Collins' lumber operation, bringing in workers' wives, children, and family stability, increasingly dimmed Little Reno's lights. Newly elected Sheriff Mel Schooler finally turned off the light. Little Reno, like Stover's rodeo, became a memory. Schooler had run on a campaign of eliminating Plumas County's illegal gambling and soon Chester became a quiet, family town. A new Chester Elementary School was built during the last two years of the 1940s and a high school was constructed in 1952.

During the 1950s, Lake Almanor Peninsula opened sale of its lots. Favorable response by new residents soon necessitated a post office. Peninsula Village Post Office opened in 1966.

A town sewer system was already established, but a water system and fire hydrants didn't become a reality for Chester until the 1960s. The present fire station was built in 1958, replacing the Quonset hut station erected after World War II. This fire station, the schools, churches, library, hospital, city park, ski hill, and movie theater all contributed to the community's well-being.

Five floods had occurred since the 1937 destructive mass of water, one year having two floods. The 1972 flood that took out the Highway 36 bridge and several houses was the last one. A federally funded $7-million flood control ditch was constructed a few years after the flood, bringing peace of mind to residents and business owners.

Plumas County's first fast food franchise, the A&W, arrived during the 1970s. Former fire chief Joe Striplin said that population and business growth during the last ten years of the twentieth century has been the most significant for Chester during his better than 50 years of town residency. Prominent among these developments are the mini-shopping center on Main Street and the Lake Almanor West subdivision.

"It was a nice little community in the old days," said Marian Malvich, Chester resident since 1916. "Any problems, people pitched in and helped. I remember the days when there were more bars than churches," she says; "now it's vice-versa."

Big Meadows has vanished. So have the dairy ranches, hay barns, waterwheels, and cattle. Long gone are the Prattville Hotel and Bunnell House, as well as Peter Olsen, Reuben and Thaddeus Stover, and Melissa Bailey. But Chester, a modern mountain town, is here to stay.

9. INDIAN VALLEY: CRESCENT MILLS, GENESEE, GREENVILLE, AND TAYLORSVILLE

Approximately 500 Maidu lived in Indian Valley at the time of the white man's arrival. Indian Valley, some 4 to 6 miles in both length and width, consists of about 22,000 acres. A thin, rectangular portion of Indian Valley that juts out from it is called the North Arm. This beautiful extension on Indian Valley's east side stretches northward for 7 miles.

Peter Lassen came to Indian Valley in 1850 looking for the fabled Gold Lake and was so impressed with the valley that he returned that fall with a number of others and built a square log cabin trading post with a brush-covered roof. The trading post was the first building erected in Indian Valley by white men. In the spring of 1851, they planted a vegetable garden that included potatoes, carrots, lettuce, turnips, beets, and cabbage, and was the first agricultural endeavor in Plumas County history.

They soon replaced the brush covering of their log house with a good roof; thus, the first building in Indian Valley stood completed. A historical monument about 3 miles north of Greenville, on the North Valley Road, marks the Lassen cabin site.

Jobe Taylor, born in Pennsylvania in 1811, decided in 1849 at age 38 to travel overland to California. After some time spent mining, he joined the Noble's party of 80 men looking for Gold Lake. In 1851, when Noble's party came to Indian Valley, they saw so many Maidu, it was decided the appropriate name for the location would be Indian Valley. While in the valley, Taylor realized the overall setting was ideal for farming.

Taylor returned to mining at Nelson Creek 10 miles southeast of Quincy, but in February 1852, decided to go back to Indian Valley where he posted a notice claiming much of the valley and the area now occupied by the town of Taylorsville.

In 1853 he planted some vegetables and grew the first wheat and barley in Indian Valley's history. He built the first barn that same year, and soon after opened a store in his home, which he also used as a hotel for travelers. The first

Taylorsville's school was built in 1864 and served the town until 1948 when it was deemed unsafe. The new one was built on the site of Jobe Taylor's Hotel. The little brick school still stands.

social event in the valley, a festive ball, was given at Taylor's home in February 1853 and the first horse races were held in his field the next year. He brought the first cat to the valley and opened the first butcher shop in August 1855. In 1854, Taylor was elected Plumas County surveyor, a job he held for one year. He built a sawmill in 1855 and a four-story gristmill in 1856. The power for his mills came from a millrace he constructed out of Indian Creek. With his business established, Jobe Taylor and Sophia Hodgkins were married in 1857 by a Justice of the Peace at Elizabethtown. Sophia was a member of the same overland party that Taylor had joined going to California in 1849.

Taylor's sawmill allowed the growing number of settlers to make frame homes instead of log cabins. His gristmill also allowed them to convert grain to flour. Taylor charged 45¢ per bushel for grinding. Besides supplying local needs, flour from Taylor's mill was shipped by pack mules to the Idaho mines during the 1860s.

Dr. Cory began practicing medicine, and in August 1852 the valley's first white child was born to a couple passing through. A voting precinct site was established at Taylor's home in the fall of 1852 for the presidential election in which Democrat Franklin Pierce won. During the same winter, Taylor built the first blacksmith shop in the valley. Growth and community pride soon elevated "Taylor's place" to "Taylorville," then in 1863 to the present Taylorsville, a quiet mountain town that has the distinction of being the longest continually occupied town in Plumas County's history, 1852 to the present.

On the Western Pacific Railroad High Line, Crescent Mills is an agricultural community with a history of logging and gold mining.

In November 1853, because of strained Native American–Anglo relations, Taylor convened a meeting at his house to work out a plan in which the grievances of both white man and Native American were to be treated the same. It was agreed by both parties that equal treatment should be meted out to both races when any injustice had been done.

A month later, on December 18, trouble of the worst kind erupted. George Rose, a blacksmith, entered Taylor's hotel. Near the stove was seated an old Native American. On noticing him, Rose asked Taylor, "What business has that Indian in this house?" Taylor replied that he was a good man who only wanted to get warm. Rose was not satisfied and walked up to the Native American, pulled his revolver, and shot him dead, then made a fast exit from the hotel and rode home. The next day, a posse of settlers went to Rose's home 3 miles away to arrest him. Rose resisted, but the posse subdued him and took him to Taylor's ranch to hold a trial. A court was assembled consisting of a judge and 11 jurors. After the short trial, the jury found Rose guilty of murder and sentenced him to be hanged before 2 p.m. that same day. The sentence was promptly carried out.

The first marriage in Indian Valley was between Robert Ross and Mrs. Catherine Deitch and became a comical affair. Since there was no minister or proper magistrate, the couple solemnly promised in the presence of witnesses to be man and wife. Soon, they moved to Rush Creek where gold mining was going well. It was there that John Buckbee, a lawyer and miner, declared their marriage illegal and married them again. Not long thereafter, squire Thomas Bonner, a Justice of the Peace, visited the area and informed them they were still not properly married in the eyes of the law, so they were officially married by him for the third and last time.

As part of Taylorsville's growth, the Blood brothers and E.D. Hosselkus opened a new store in 1857. A private school opened in 1859 and a post office began in 1861. By that year, Taylorsville had two general stores, a butcher shop, a fruit store, blacksmith shop, livery stable, eight or ten houses, two taverns, several barns, a sawmill, a gristmill, Taylor's Hotel, and the new Vernon House Hotel. Although still without a minister or church, all the stores closed on the Sabbath, the taverns shut down, and billiard tables were covered.

Indian Valley's first public school opened at Taylorsville in 1863 and a new brick schoolhouse that is still standing was built in 1864. Sunday school services began in 1864 and the brick store that would become George Young's Market was also built that year. A Masonic Lodge opened in 1867 over Young's store, and the Independent Order of Odd Fellows (IOOF) Lodge hall was completed that same year over Rosenburg's brick store.

During the 1870s, water was brought in from Montgomery Creek, 2.5 miles away, for fire protection. This improvement arrived just in time, for in March 1875, a destructive Saturday night fire caused $5,000 in damage. Among the buildings destroyed was that used for church purposes. A subscription was quickly taken up, and the new Methodist-Episcopal church was finished in December 1875. It has the distinction of being the second oldest church in the county and the longest still standing.

Taylorsville was reaching its population plateau during the years between the 1870s and the 1920s. For nearly two decades, Taylorsville was the main north-south point between Indian Valley and American Valley. During the 1870s the new American Valley–Indian Valley Road was constructed, bypassing Taylorsville. The Red Clover Wagon Road was finished by 1873 and allowed traffic through Taylorsville to Genesee Valley, Red Clover Valley, Sierra Valley, Beckwourth Pass, and on to Reno. Indian Valley ranchers found this a more favorable route than Chico for their shipments of butter.

Andrew John Hickerson took up Peter Lassen's land when the latter left the valley around 1854. The first bridge crossing Indian Creek was built in 1853 and the Fargo, Singer Express Company began operating that same year. The Schaffer brothers planted the first fruit trees in the valley in 1854.

By 1861, the valley had 50 farms and ranches covering 14,000 acres. In 1866, Indian Valley's total agricultural value for the year was $150,000. According to the newspaper, "Every farmer in the valley has his granaries filled to overflowing, his barns filled with the finest quality of hay, and his root houses crowded with the choicest vegetables."

Levi Hunt was among those Indian Valley ranchers in the 1860s. Finding gold was his dream when he first passed through Indian Valley in 1855, but after time spent pursuing mining, he settled on a 377-acre ranch in east-central Indian Valley. Levi developed and enjoyed a self-subsistent frontier ranching life, raising vegetables, grain, hay, horses, and cattle, and operating a small dairy.

Levi's son Asa took over the ranch when his father died at age 80. Asa continued his father's diversified farming methods, while increasing the number of dairy cows. His son Elmore followed in his footsteps until he moved to Greenville. For more than 138 years, the Hunt family continuously lived and farmed in Indian Valley.

Gold was the metal that economically anchored Greenville and Indian Valley's foundation from the 1850s to the turn of the century. Placer yields at Wolf and Lights Creeks were encouraging during the 1850s and a hard rock mine named the Bullion was discovered near what became the town of Greenville in 1851. A second quartz mine called the Lone Star was discovered in 1857. Excitement generated by this new discovery helped develop other prospects in the area.

Entrepreneurial Mrs. Green knew that because of the influx of miners, various services were needed. She served them tasty, home-cooked meals at her log cabin in the northwestern corner of the valley. Her meals were so well appreciated, her residence was soon known as Green's Hotel.

In the spring of 1860, two transient miners named Palmer and Newlands found an extremely rich placer field at Round Valley, 1 mile from and more than 1,000 feet above the Indian Valley floor. The news of their good fortune spread like wildfire and miners from all over swarmed to the site.

John Ellis added to the excitement when he found an outcropping that warranted construction of a 24-stamp mill. Nearly 400 miners tossed up canvas and log dwellings, and soon a hotel, four saloons, three stores, gambling dens, and a livery stable followed. Almost immediately, these were augmented by two sawmills, a Wells, Fargo and Company express office, and a school. Round Valley blossomed into a real town.

In order to create enough water for mining, it was decided to build a dam at the outlet of Round Valley at the head of North Canyon. In 1861, the first dam was built, but broke. A second dam built in 1862 also broke, but the third dam, built in 1864, was substantial enough to hold. Because of Round Valley's location high on the mountain, it was inconvenient for wagon traffic. It wasn't long before businesses moved down the mountain and located near Green's Hotel, giving birth to the town of Greenville. The exact year of this event is not clear, and little is known of the Greens. A second home was built near the Green Hotel by Alfred McCarger in 1861 or 1862. McCarger was the owner of the nearby Bullion Mine. Henry C. Bidwell moved his family to the new settlement of Greenville in 1862. Within a short period, a handful of others decided to settle in that area also.

Greenville's birth, settlement, and economic prosperity were all a direct result of Round Valley's mineral riches. Round Valley's rich placers were the beginning of the discovery of two dozen new quartz mines in the following 20 years in what became known as the Greenville Mining District.

Among the most productive of the hard rock mines was the Green Mountain Mine with six tunnels reaching depths of 250 feet and lengths of 6,075 feet. Its 75 employees fed ore to the 92 stamps at its mill, powered by water supplied from Round Valley Lake.

The Gold Digger's Parade has been held in downtown Greenville almost every year since this photograph was taken in June, 1941.

Other quartz mines producing equally rich yields were the Union and Indian Valley mines, with 56 stamps. The Gold Stripe and Plumas each had 30 stamps. For 30 years, the Crescent Mine, discovered in 1864, was worked by a 32-stamp mill paying $8 to $12 per ton. The New York, Kittle (the Cherokee group of mines), Indian Valley, Southern Eureka, Taylor Plumas, and Arcadia each had 10 to 20 stamps pounding away. The two dozen hard rock mines throughout the Greenville Mining District had a combined total of 314 stamps.

Henry C. Bidwell was an entrepreneur and one of the most esteemed citizens of Greenville during the nineteenth century. Bidwell came to Plumas County in 1860 and spent 20 years of his life specializing in mining matters. At the time of his death in 1880, he was president of the Green Mountain Mine, the Cherokee Mining Company, and the Gold Stripe Mine on Wolf Creek.

Colonel Bidwell, as he was known, was born in Vermont in 1831. At the age of 17, he left home to fight in the Mexican-American War. One year later, in 1849, he traveled by ship to San Francisco. For several years, he was engaged in steam boating and merchandising until he came to Plumas County. During his 20 years of mining, it was said he met "with alternate successes and reversals at first, but recently has been eminently successful." He was a community-minded man and started the Round Valley Reservoir Company to supply water to Greenville.

The first town school was organized in 1865. Classroom instruction was first held in a hotel room, but within a year the school was moved into a room over a town saloon. When a shooting fracas occurred and an errant bullet came up through the floor, the local citizens promptly moved the school site off the main street. Hattie Fairchild became the teacher at the new school, which opened during the winter of 1866–1867 at what was described as "the first good school we have had here for a long time, numbering some twenty pupils." Greenville's first post office also opened in 1867.

Charles H. Lawrence was born in Pennsylvania in 1832, and at the age of 27 traveled overland to California. By the following year (1860), he had built a sawmill in Round Valley, which he operated for four years. In 1864 he moved to Greenville and built a home. He also constructed a livery stable as a way to make a living. His stable proved a success, and being young and ambitious, he soon erected a flourmill, started the town's first foundry, and opened a tin shop. In 1870, he began two new sawmill operations, and using his mill's lumber, he built the Greenville Hotel. In six years, Lawrence had become one of Greenville's most substantial citizens. As time progressed, he acquired 1,000 acres of Indian Valley lands, a hotel in Quincy, and an American Valley farm.

Meanwhile, development was occurring at the new town of Crescent Mills, located in a picturesque dell in the southwestern edge of Indian Valley. Gold was the primary impetus leading to Crescent Mills's beginning, just as it was for Greenville. The primary difference between the two towns was the swiftness of settlement. Greenville grew rapidly as a supply center for the Round Valley placer mines. Crescent Mills's growth was slower.

The Wheelock Ranch barn on the North Valley Road in Indian Valley was a landmark until it fell during the winter of 1993. Hay was stored in barns like this one all over Indian Valley for winter feed for the ranchers' livestock.

The two largest, most productive hard rock mines discovered in the immediate Crescent Mills area were the Green Mountain Mine in 1860 and the Crescent Mine in 1864. Several smaller lodes occasionally proved profitable. For most of the 30-year period from the 1870s to the 1890s, Crescent Mills enjoyed its most populous and financially lucrative years. The first house was built during the winter of 1860 and 1861 by J.W. Pulsifer, a local mine owner. Mathias Knoll's brewery opened the next year and 36 residents voted at the first polls held in 1868.

By the 1870s, a huge boarding house was built where 100 miners slept and ate. Seven saloons helped occupy their idle time. A restaurant and blacksmith shop were opened in 1877 and another two-story building was going up. George Tanner, a miner during much of the 1870s through the 1900s, said Crescent Mills had 500 miners working in the underground mines and living in town. Those living in the large boarding house built by John J. Fisher during the 1890s paid $3 a day for room and board.

The earliest kindergarten through eighth grade school had to be replaced in 1889 by a larger primary and grammar school where 60 students studied reading, writing, arithmetic, and penmanship five days a week. Sunday school was held in the same institution of learning.

In 1876, the entirely new Wolf Creek Quartz Mining District, 5 miles west of Greenville, emerged. A February 1877 *Plumas National Bulletin* account reported the lodes "in this newly discovered locality are developing magnificently from nearly all the claims on which work is being done." During the last three years of the 1870s, Wolf Creek quartz mines became "the most prosperous region in the area."

East across the valley and up Indian Creek, Bidwell's Lebanon Mine in Genesee engaged ten men, and the Genesee Mine, first opened in 1859 using hydraulic mining, was now maintaining its quartz operations.

The Greenville Foundry was among the town businesses taking full advantage of the "bull market," casting shoes and dies, and making stoves and hardware items. Two steam sawmills were kept busy. W. Stevens had two extra men employed in his blacksmith shop. McIntyre and Company's immense stock of goods was selling fast. Clothing and dry goods were selling well at Sternberg's new store. John McBeth opened a new store and the Maxwell Hotel was going "full blast," as the town was overflowing with people. Fully loaded stages, including John Hardgrave's twice-a-week runs to Reno, were regularly bringing miners and opportunists from all points.

New buildings were rapidly being constructed, 20 new structures being put up in June 1877. During May and June of that same year, eight new businesses opened: a tin shop, boot and shoe store, millinery shop, jewelry and music store, barbershop, drugstore, and harness shop. Plumas County's first bank had been opened earlier during the year by M. Perine. Greenville's population doubled between 1877 and 1878.

Growth during the decade increased the number of town blacksmiths to three, barbers to three, butchers to two, and several more saloons opened. Erection of the county's first Methodist church was begun in June 1873 and services were soon being held there. At George Proctor's two-story Greenville Hotel, the largest building in town, he regularly had 50 to 100 boarders. H.C. Bidwell (who had sent the town's first telegram in 1874) organized the Round Valley Water Company in 1876. By the following summer, John McBeth and J.D. Compton were building a town reservoir, "thirty-six feet high with a capacity of about ten thousand gallons."

By 1882, Greenville boasted a population of about 500 people, second only to Quincy, with Taylorsville and Crescent Mills next. Despite a brutal fire in April 1881, the town could still boast one large hotel, three stores, restaurants, saloons, market, barbers, boarding house, soda factory, dentist, physician, foundry, flour mill, sawmill, livery stable, blacksmiths, shoemaker, wagon maker, upholstery shop, Methodist church, school, telegraph service, post office, express office, newspaper, water works, and several fraternal organizations.

Winter snows began in late October and could be 3 feet deep on Indian Valley's meadowlands by Christmas. During peak snowfalls, it sometimes reached a depth of 7 feet on the valley floor. The melting snows and spring rains sometimes caused floods, as they did in 1907 when 3 feet of water hit some of the valley's homes.

Although gold production within the Greenville Mining District began to wane during the 1890s, Indian Valley's population continued to grow. A new school was built in Crescent Mills in 1889 and Greenville's second school replaced the original one in 1910. Teacher Mary Schieser recalled having more than 40 students in her Greenville primary class in 1893. A pioneer telephone system was in operation in 1885 from Crescent Mills to Greenville via a half-dozen quartz mines. A Catholic church was built in Greenville in 1893, but for the preceding 30 years, masses were limited to three per year, a priest coming by horse and buggy from Truckee.

By 1900, the Greenville Hotel and livery stable on Main Street took up nearly an entire block, and William Hall had started a general merchandise store.

As many as 100 or more Chinese lived in Greenville where a fairly large Chinatown existed on the west side of Wolf Creek. Among the buildings was a big saloon, a Chinese store, and a bathhouse.

Approximately 250 of the estimated original 500 Maidu still lived in Indian Valley, Genesee Valley, and the surrounding mountains in 1900. A federally funded government Greenville Indian School was built in 1888 to serve as a day school for Indian Valley Native Americans and a boarding school for all other tribes in northern California. This building burned down in 1897, was replaced in 1898 with a larger facility, then burned again in 1921 and was never rebuilt.

Between World War I and World War II the timber industry added to the growth of the area economy. Three or four sawmills had been opened between the turn of the century and World War II. Prominent among them were Fred Farrar's sawmill near Indian Falls, which he moved to Peck's Valley around 1910; the Indian Falls Mill (1908–1927) and the Donnenwirth Mill at Taylorsville near today's rodeo grounds (1917–1924); the Taresh Brother's Mill, which took over the Donnenwirth Mill when it burned in 1924; as well as the Phippen Brother's Mill on the old Hunt Ranch in Indian Valley (1926–1931). The Phippens were the first to use log trucks in lumber operations in the Indian Valley area. Elmore Hunt was the first driver of the 5-ton solid tire White logging trucks.

Foremost of the sawmills operating during the depression decade was the new Setzer Box Company on the west side of Wolf Creek that opened in 1934. A 45-man work crew was employed at the sawmill where 125,000 board feet were cut each eight-hour working day. One hundred Setzer woodsmen toiled in the woods falling, bucking, and moving the trees to the Setzer plant's 2-acre millpond. Greenville began growing south and west to its present town dimensions during the last half of the 1930s. Setzer Box Company was the main reason for the housing on the west side of Wolf Creek.

Camille Frizzie operated two sawmills during the depression decade, one at his Dixie Canyon plant and a new one at Crescent Mills following completion of the WPRR High Line. Frizzie's Crescent Mills plant operated until World War II, cutting about 50,000 board feet a day.

Mike Ayoob finished construction of a new two-story hotel on the corner of Main and Crescent Streets in August 1931. Three blocks of Main Street were graded with crushed rock and oiled in a 40-foot-wide strip in the spring of 1933.

The old Hosselkus home in Genesee still stands opposite the Genesee store in the shadow of the snow-covered Grizzly Ridge, 6 miles west of Taylorsville.

These historic buildings still stand at the corner of Main Street and Highway 89 in Greenville, though the occupants have changed since this photograph was taken in 1882.

When President Franklin Delano Roosevelt raised gold's price 43 percent from $20.67 to $35 an ounce by the Gold Reserve Act of 1934, it instantly re-stimulated Indian Valley mining. The Standart, New York, and Arcadia were soon going full speed. The Standart was purchased in 1933 by Indian Valley Mining Company from F.J. Standart, son of the mine's discoverer, Frank Standart, one of the mining pioneers of the region. By October 1937, progress was going so well in the Standart Mine at its new lower Eureka Vein, 1,000 feet below the Southern Eureka, that the *Indian Valley Record* was prompted to write, "the mine may become one of the largest operations in the state." Three shifts were working and a new mill was acquired by 1938 with a 150-ton daily capacity. On March 2, 1939, it burned to the ground. By mid-August, a new mill was up, the "most modern gold mining plant in the world." World War II shut it down.

The Indian Valley mine, 1.5 miles south of Greenville, where 2 million dollars had been extracted around the turn of the century, was reopened in June 1934 and the Green Mountain Mine at Crescent Mills reopened in October 1934 with a six to eight man work crew. Meanwhile, the crew at the Lucky S quartz mine in the mountains a few miles east of the North Arm hit hard rock ore worth $50 per ton gross yield, $36 net after shipping and expenses.

Electrical service had begun in Greenville and Crescent Mills in the summer of 1909. Power to provide electricity was generated by a 60-horsepower hydro plant in Greenville where falling water was received from a reservoir above the town. If the water supply dropped too low, the lights went off, thus restricting electrical usage to certain hours. Eighty-four customers were being served by 1915 and Taylorsville's electrical service began in 1917.

Electric service to rural Indian Valley ranchers was delayed for a decade, until Donald J. McIntyre purchased a Great Western Power Company subsidiary utility in 1922 at sheriff's sale and began service. Radios arrived in the 1920s and a movie theater by 1930.

Judge Hamblin's Ford agency in downtown Greenville was the center of interest in 1912. Bob Cooke well remembered his first 45-minute ride from Taylorsville to Greenville the same year, chugging along at an average speed of about 15 miles per hour. When Elmore Hunt drove his first Model T Ford in 1918, there were probably less than 50 automobiles in Plumas County.

Roads, of course, were all dirt in the World War I era and mostly dirt with occasional stretches of crushed gravel until World War II. Snowplows were unheard of. Mud-soaked Main Street would "almost mire down a horse and wagon," remembered Elmore Hunt, and to cross it by foot in winter you needed "knee high boots," agreed Charlie Walters.

Bob Gott's first automobile ride from Greenville to Quincy in 1923 took two hours. Ralph and Ruby Lozano laughed while remembering that if they wanted to go to Quincy for any reason, you just set aside "the whole day."

During the summer in the 1920s and 1930s, Saturday night dances were held once a month in Greenville and Taylorsville. At the Taylorsville Grange Hall, the floor joists had been constructed in a manner that enabled dancers to enjoy their evening of dancing in such delightful bouncing that they called it a "spring floor."

Old timers had never forgotten the 1881 fire in Greenville that had destroyed nearly the entire town. A town fire department had been organized shortly thereafter. Disaster was contained for three or four decades until it reared its ugly head again in June 1918 and burned down much of the northern business half of Taylorsville. The Greenville Hotel burned to the ground in 1922. In September 1926, more than half the town of Crescent Mills—34 buildings—was destroyed by an arsonist. Plumas County deputy sheriff Stacy Baccala, also Greenville's fire chief, didn't want it to happen again. When a bootlegger's Ford truck was confiscated by the authorities in 1931, Baccala and the Greenville Fire Department bought it. By the next year, they had it converted into a workable fire engine.

A new library was built in 1952; a new hospital, paved roads, and dial telephones also arrived in the 1950s. In 1955, First Western Bank purchased the Indian Valley Bank started in 1912 by Dick and Cecilia M. Chamberlain.

A shopping center was constructed next to Highway 89 in the southern part of Greenville in 1965. PG&E purchased Indian Valley Light and Power in 1966. Before the decade had ended, Greenville's dimensions had doubled that of 100 years before.

Margaret Cooke started a quilting club in 1957 at the Taylorsville Community United Methodist Church. Women met all day on Tuesdays and Thursdays to make quilts, chat at random while quilting, socialize, drink coffee, and share potluck lunches. Beautiful finished quilts are sold at their annual May Quilt Show and October Fall Festival. All proceeds from the sales are used for needy community projects and families. Word spread of their painstaking work and small-town togetherness. In the spring, the *Los Angeles Times* ran an article about the quilting club and NBC featured the ladies and their beautiful quilts on national television. For summer entertainment, the Silver Buckle Rodeo was inaugurated at Taylorsville in 1949 and continues to this day. Diane Fisher was the first Queen of the Silver Buckle Rodeo in 1952. A community swimming pool was built in the mid-1960s. Volunteers finished one of the town's greatest assets, the Mt. Jura Gem and Mineral Society and Indian Valley Museum facility in 1973.

Over time, Indian Valley has suffered a number of economic reversals. Indian Valley's dairy ranching died in 1965. Cal-Vada Lumber Company closed its sawmill in 1957. Meadow Valley Lumber Company and Setzer Box Company shut down in 1963 and 1968. Cheney Lumber ceased operations in 1975. Louisiana Pacific closed its doors in 1979, leaving 75 workers unemployed. In 1983, their Crescent Mills plant went on strike, closing permanently. WPRR closed its Greenville depot in 1974. Ayoob's clothing store shut down in 1985 and the town movie theater soon followed suit. First Interstate Bank locked its doors in 1987, a year after the Plumas Bank opened.

With fewer jobs and less opportunities, young folks finished high school and then went off to college or moved away to find a job. Some residents want progress and growth. Others appreciate their comforts: a sufficient number of services, fewer crowds, a small population, clean air, and magnificent, awe-inspiring beauty.

Named for its founder Jobe Taylor, Taylorsville is noted for its rural ambiance and fertile farmland; note the barns throughout town and the church established in 1875.

10. Sierra Valley & Eastern Plumas: Beckwourth, Mohawk Valley, and Portola

Portola's history is one of trains and trees. The first white man to purposely arrive at what became the town of Portola came in 1886. He was a surveyor employed by SV&MRR, which was organized in 1885 by the California Land and Timber Company, holders of vast tracts of forestland in eastern Plumas and Sierra Counties. Their objective was to build sawmills and a railroad line into Plumas County. These were the initial steps that would lead to the founding of the town of Portola. However, it wasn't until 1895 that SVRR's tracks passed through present-day Portola, then known as Mormon Junction.

Around 1900, various lumber companies had been purchasing sections of federal timberland in the Portola area, some for $1.25 per acre. The B&L laid tracks northwest from Loyalton in 1902 to Beckwourth, near Grizzly Creek, and back across the Middle Fork to Rocky Point. They then paralleled the south side of the river to Portola to about 100 yards south of the present-day overpass. Spur tracks continued to where the Union Pacific station now stands, then around the mountain into the canyon where a White Pine Lumber Company loading dock stood. White Pine's 90 employees lived in tents from the season's start in April until winter storms began. Eight-year-old Uldene Long Fonda's family lived there year round in a little wood cabin for five years. Mrs. Long acted as the company cook and Mr. Long was the butcher. This pioneer logging camp was Portola's foundation.

The WPRR was officially organized in 1903 to become the nation's sixth transcontinental railroad line. WPRR management decided Portola would be an ideal site for one of their construction camps and established "Headquarters," with living quarters for the crews, equipment sheds, and a commissary. Headquarters was not a popular name, so it was changed to Imola, then Reposa, and finally Portola. Its present name is thought to have been suggested by Virgilia Bogue, daughter of WPRR official Virgil Bogue in honor of Spanish explorer Gaspar de Portola.

Charles Gulling of Reno Mill and Lumber Company laid out the original Portola town site in 1909 with the assistance of the Roberts Lumber Company. A local group known as the Portola Development Company became active in town development needs. Numerous houses were built, Portola Development Company constructed rental cabins, and there was a grocery store, a restaurant, and half a dozen business shops. E. Treesdale opened a "Ladies and Gents strictly up to date" clothing, shoe, and boot store, advertised as "one of the largest stores in the county." Water was hauled in barrels from the spring above the present high school. A post office also opened in 1909 and a private grammar school opened its doors that same year in James Harris's home on the north side of the river. Students had to ford the Feather River at its shallowest point, below the present Veterans Hall. In 1910, Reno Mill and Lumber Company built a wooden truss bridge across the river, permitting the children a safe crossing to and from school. According to Belle Quigley Branstetter, average daily attendance was about 21 students. Branstetter received an annual salary of $437. During her year of teaching, she rented a four-room, partly tent boarding house. Portola's first permanent grammar school was built in 1911 on today's Beckwith Street near Highway 70.

By April of 1910, Portola had a population of 400 people, including more than 100 railroad employees. By 1911, downtown Portola boasted nearly a dozen stores, several restaurants, a barbershop equipped with baths, a jewelry store, drugstore, and a lodging home. Two new lumber mills were erected in the town suburbs in 1910 and WPRR opened a community hospital that same year.

Portola became a town with the construction of the Western Pacific Railroad. It is situated along the banks of the Feather River Middle Fork headwaters. This photograph was taken c. 1910.

Portola's founding fathers informed WPRR management that they would agree to prohibition measures in exchange for Portola's becoming the division point rather than the heavily salooned Beckwourth. They knew Beckwourth with its dozen saloons was the primary culprit in the absenteeism of WPRR employees. Beckwourth, whose beginnings include the famous Jim Beckwourth, grew as a result of Sierra Valley farming, the Clover Valley Road, and the SVRR. Misnamed Beckwith by the post office in 1870, the spelling was corrected in 1932.

When the SVRR reached Beckwourth in 1895, the town began its most prosperous years. Beckwourth became the primary railroad import-export center of Plumas County. Stagecoaches, teamsters, and railroad men were busy with the increased commerce. Over time, and after several fires, the town has returned to its original sleepy existence.

As a division point, Portola rapidly became the region's trade center. By 1912, Charles Gulling began his new hotel, and a livery stable, box factory, ice plant, opera house, jewelry store, and Reiser Hall—a community meeting place—all came into being. A fire hose cart was obtained about this time and housed in a little shed beneath a fire bell next to Storrs Street. By 1913, the population reached 600 and talks began for incorporation. Jack Schill's new movie theater-nickelodeon opened in 1917. A cement dam was built to enable ice to be harvested from the river and the site became an extremely popular community ice skating arena.

A new steel bridge crossing the Middle Fork of the Feather River was constructed in 1922, replacing the wooden one that had been built in 1910. Rich copper deposits at Walker Mine, located 10 miles northwest of Portola, added to the economic growth of the town during the 1920s and 1930s.

Throughout that time, residents from the mine swarmed to Portola on weekends. After cashing their paychecks, they spent freely at grocery stores, clothing shops, and at Schill, Reynolds & Jones's combination meat, groceries, clothing, saloon, pool hall, and card room. This latter place is most remembered following its ownership transfer in 1930 as the HM&J Club (Hoxey, McGowan and Janes). Undesirables were disrupting the peaceful air of the young town. It was said, "No lady walked on the north side of Commercial Street." From the beginning, Portola was a wide open town where "every other door was a bar or saloon." Bootlegging, gambling, and houses of prostitution headed the list of recreational activities. Craps, cards, and slot machines became ordinary Commercial Street activities. These activities led to meetings by the Portola Improvement Club "to drive all objectionable characters out of the city."

The majority of residents in the 1920s, of course, lived a more orderly life. In 1917, James Turner gave the Methodist church a larger building for services and moved it to a site above the present church, adding a parsonage. Church membership increased, and the present Methodist Church was built in 1949.

An elementary school was built in 1921 and, by 1925, a new $20,000 K-12 school was built. Unfortunately, the school burned down its opening year, but rebuilding occurred rapidly and classes resumed as before.

Portola, once a division point for the Western Pacific Railroad, sprang up in 1909 and began to flourish immediately. Commercial Street is its main business district, shown here in 1945. It was said in the early years that "no lady walked on the north side of Commercial Street."

In 1927, the Portola Water Company became a public utility when the town acquired Gulling's waterworks. Two blocks on Commercial Street were paved with concrete in 1928 and strips of gravel were dumped at more heavily traveled crossings during the muddy winter season.

In late August of 1928, the most ruinous blaze in the town's history occurred, wiping out an entire business block in downtown Portola. Six Commercial Street stores were destroyed as well as ten dwellings. Among the businesses burned were a bakery, laundry, cafe, pool hall, the Golden Hotel, and Grizzly Electric Company office.

In 1931, the town acquired its first fire engine and a new fire station was built in 1937 on Nevada Street.

During the early 1930s, North Side Grocery opened as the first retail store north of the Middle Fork. The Memorial Hall was built by citizens in 1937 at a cost of $26,000. The new structure was an immediate success, hosting events ranging from dances to weddings. The town's second and more modern fire station was constructed in 1941 at the corner of First Avenue and Pacific Street. Rural Electric service was brought into the area as well.

Up to the 1940s, bootlegging, gambling, and red light houses such as the Seven Steps, Green Lantern, and Willow Glen continued business in Portola, Beckwourth, and vicinity. Beckwourth alone had seven red light houses operating

134

simultaneously during the 1930s. According to a lifetime Portola resident, Hap Manit, at one time during the 1930s, there were nine churches, nine saloons, and nine houses of prostitution.

In 1946, Portola residents incorporated their city of 1,500 to gain more local control. Several new churches were constructed as city population reached 2,000. Residential streets were paved in the early 1950s. Fire protection and traffic flow was improved when the Gulling Street overpass was constructed in 1953. More stores and homes were built on the north side of the river. The year 1955 brought dial telephones, television, completion of the new Portola pool, and development of the Portola Park.

Frenchman Lake was completed in 1961 and Lake Davis followed in 1966. Davis became an anglers' favorite. As many as 8,000 visitors came to the lake on opening weekend of fishing season in May 1968. Due to an infestation of Northern Pike, in 1997, Department of Fish and Game poisoned the lake with Rotenone. It has since recovered, but unfortunately, so have the pike.

Lester Davis was a WPRR engineer and, in 1946, the first Portola resident to be elected to the California state legislature. Davis, a Democrat, served seven years before his death in 1952. Lake Davis is named after him. Pauline Davis, Lester's wife, succeeded him and served 11 more terms, from 1952 to 1976, gaining the distinction of serving the longest time in the state assembly, 24 years, of any woman legislator.

As a member of the state legislature, Pauline Davis was an avid supporter of local control in government and was one of the prime movers of the State Water Plan, which included the creation of Antelope Reservoir, Frenchman Reservoir, and Lake Davis. State Lieutenant Governor Leo McCarthy called Pauline Davis "the most effective legislator in representing her district's special needs that I have ever seen. She used up-front direct confrontation while so doing, but was always a lady about it."

Clair Donnenwirth was born in Taylorsville on September 9, 1906. He was Portola's most effective Plumas County supervisor, serving for 16 years, from 1948 to 1965. Among the measures he is credited with are the campaign to incorporate Portola; the Gulling Street overpass; active support for development of the Upper Feather River Water Projects; establishment of Plumas-Eureka State Park; and miscellaneous contributions for improvement of local and county streets, highways, schools, libraries, and public buildings.

Upon her husband's death in 1965, Dorothy Donnenwirth was appointed Plumas County supervisor by Governor Pat Brown. She was re-elected two more terms until retiring in 1978. She was the first woman supervisor in Plumas County's history and, at the time, one of only three or four in the entire state.

For almost a century, beginning in 1909, Portola has been a railroad town. Most residents stay because they love their small Sierra Nevada mountain town. The Portola Railroad Museum, the William's House Museum, and the Jim Beckwourth Cabin Museum house many of the artifacts of Portola and Sierra Valley's vibrant past.

Farmers followed the gold miners of 1851 to Mohawk Valley. George and Robert Penman, George McLear, Thomas Wash, William Knott, G.W. Meylert, and John McKenzie were among the early ones to establish ranches. The meadows were ideal for beef and dairy cattle, providing plenty of hay for feed and fertile soil for raising wheat, potatoes, and hardy vegetables. Nearly all the Mohawk Valley residents were farmers. Not until 1884, the year of Knickrem's arrival, were there enough people to warrant establishment of voting precincts at Mohawk and McLears.

In 1884, newly arrived J.C. Knickrem set up a sawmill a mile from Mohawk. Knickrem was one of the earliest large sawmill operators at Mohawk by the 1890s. During the mid-1890s, he was cutting 25,000 board feet a day. Later, he built another sawmill west of the present-day Plumas-Eureka subdivision and golf course.

Clio became the primary Mohawk Valley timber center in 1903 when the NCO extended its line there. By 1907, mills at Clio included the Clio Lumber Company, the McKenzie Mill, and the Burkhard and Gracey Mill. McKenzie's was a large modern plant, cutting 40,000 feet per day, while Clio Lumber Company, by 1917, was cutting 6 million feet a year.

Arthur Davies arrived in Mohawk Valley in 1916 and acquired a 12,000-acre timber tract stretching from Blairsden to Calpine. At the time, Davies also owned

Like the rest of the country, Plumas County enjoyed baseball mania. Teams from the various communities played each other on Sunday afternoons, with a large picnic usually following. Here is the Portola Baseball Team on Commercial Street in 1913.

a sawmill operation in Sardine Valley, as well as a Delleker sawmill, from which most of the nearby harvestable timber had already been cut.

Arthur Davies built his new sawmill in June 1916 a short distance behind the present-day grocery store. Using a modern single bandsaw, the new plant was cutting about 50,000 board feet a day. Roughly 90 percent of the lumber was pine. A rail spur line was constructed from Davies' Mill to Clio from where the NCO line continued on to Reno. WPRR also built a 1-mile spur line in 1916 from Blairsden to Davies' Mill. In February 1917, a fire destroyed the mill, but it was rapidly replaced and cut 13 to 14 million feet of timber in 1917.

Davies moved his company houses at Sardine Valley to his new mill. The homes were sawn in half so they would fit on B&L flatcars, then moved by rail to Beckwourth, where they were transferred to NCO flatcars and carried to Clio. From this point, horses and wagons or trucks moved them to Graeagle. Davies also moved a few vacant dwellings from Clairville and Delleker by placing logs under each to serve as a frame base, then placed the entire dwelling on giant wheels, which transported them either by horse teams or Mack trucks to Graeagle. A rooming house for bachelors was erected near the lumberyard and rows of two-man cabins were built near the millpond and Gray Eagle Creek. An excellent cookhouse was built east of the millpond that featured a workingman's dining room that was the envy of the area. Davies next created a large dairy where the current stables are located. His milk and beef cattle roamed the meadows. His company store followed, selling milk, butter, cheese, fresh meat, and groceries of all kinds.

A regular little community was growing around the mill. The jobs paid well and individual needs were being met. In July 1918, the Davies Mill post office opened. California Fruit Exchange of Sacramento liked what they saw and offered Davies $1 million. He took it.

California Fruit Exchange needed lots of lumber to make the thousands of fruit boxes used each year for transporting Sacramento Valley fruit via the WPRR to the east coast markets. When the deal closed in 1919, the final price had risen to $1.25 million for the Davies mill complex. There was estimated to be 215 million board feet of timber, a sufficient supply to operate the mill for 30 years. California Fruit Exchange then constructed a millpond, built more housing for its employees, and changed the name of the town.

California Fruit Exchange administrators asked company employees to choose the new name. Belle Burn, daughter-in-law of Mrs. Arthur Davies, who liked the name of Gray Eagle Creek, dropped the "y" and submitted the winning entry. She won a $25 prize.

On May 20, 1920, Davies Mill Post Office was officially changed to Graeagle Post Office. California Fruit Exchange management simultaneously changed their name to Graeagle Lumber Company.

A molding mill, a planing mill, and dry kilns were soon built, as was a large boiler adjacent to the mill for generating steam power. For the single men, a second large boarding house was built. A few years later, a third boarding house was built for both bachelors and married couples. Family homes were built beginning in 1920 along Main Street. Ten or twelve more company dwellings were located at the present town park. Seasonal employees used the open flatland on the west side of Highway 89 and the south side of Gray Eagle Creek as a tent city in the early years.

During the first three years of Fruit Exchange ownership, new business shops were built in town near the grocery store. A hardware store and a butcher shop with a sawdust floor were built nearby. A slaughterhouse soon followed.

Fresh milk was delivered daily from the dairy to family homes and the cookhouse. Meals from the company's nearly self-subsistent agricultural and pastureland were served to the lumbermen at the cookhouse: bacon, sausage, ham, eggs, hotcakes, fruit, and homemade pies for breakfast, with lunches and suppers of similar size and quantity. The company cookhouse building where the men ate is known today as the Knotty Pine restaurant. A pool table, barbershop, upstairs beauty parlor, and adjoining ice cream parlor completed the structure.

Garbage was picked up daily by a horse-drawn cart as Fruit Exchange management insisted Graeagle be "the cleanest place around." The original garbage cart sits now in the front yard of "Movin' West" trailer park in town.

A stock of 18 million feet of timber was cut the first two to three years of new ownership, all from within 2.5 miles of the mill. Logs were delivered to the millpond by company owned railroad or by 7.5-ton, solid rubber-tired Mack trucks over newly constructed dirt logging roads.

Supervising these improvements and directing the overall timber operations was company manager Mr. Mortenson. Herb Rowe replaced him in late 1922 as the Graeagle manager. In 1925, Rowe extended the standard gauge rail line several miles west of Mohawk toward Smith Lake and Johnsville. Each flatcar on the logging train carried approximately 10,000 feet. Orren Barton was the first locomotive engineer.

By 1922, there were close to 600 woods and sawmill workers, wives, and children living at Graeagle, where the mill was cutting 70,000 feet daily during its ten-hour workday. Operating six, sometimes seven days a week, production numbers eventually increased to 115,000 feet a day. Everyone in the lumber camp woke up at 6 a.m. when the Fruit Exchange whistle blew and reported for work at 7 a.m. Every day for 35 years, the whistle blew for the Graeagle Lumber Company workers. When the whistle blew unexpectedly on December 7, 1922, it was because a fire was in the process of destroying the store, club, and theater.

By mid-summer 1923, construction of the still standing, although damaged, Graeagle grocery store and Knotty Pine tavern was completed. Nearly 500 people attended the August dedication ball, "the largest gathering of guests and visitors in the history of similar affairs within the county."

Graeagle's hard working men put in ten hour days six days a week at the Graeagle mill or in the woods. Sharing long working hours at home were wives cooking on wood stoves, heating water for baths, or laundering the family clothes on washboards. Lucy Vernazza, Mary McClaskey, and Nellie Miller vividly remember washing their spouses' clothes that way. Among their husbands' working attire were striped hickory shirts and tan pants of heavy canvas material that, after washing, "you could stand up at night and jump right in them in the morning."

Once a month during the 1920s and 1930s, Saturday night dances were held at the company dance hall where today's restaurant is located. Here they danced to the Sierra Syncopators, one of the top bands in northern California, plus bands from Reno and even San Francisco. Occasionally, silent movies were shown above the clubhouse and a piano was available for playing and singing.

Prizefights were held twice a month, providing summer entertainment. Top sluggers came from all over northern California, even from as far away as Salt Lake City. A town baseball team was organized for eastern Plumas County competition.

At Christmas, California Fruit Exchange gave every family a free turkey. Bachelors were given free turkey dinners at both Thanksgiving and Christmas. A large community Christmas tree was lavishly decorated each Yuletide season throughout the Fruit Exchange years. Each child was given an orange, a sack of nuts, and a toy.

Children attended the two-room Horace Mann School on Main Street that is still standing. The primary grade teacher offered learning in first through fourth grades to 20 or 25 children, while the other instructor taught a like number in grades five through eight. The PTA was an extremely enthusiastic group,

This row of little red buildings was moved by train to its present location when the Davies Mill began operations in 1916.

encouraging academic assistance and making costumes for school plays. Some students went on to high school in Portola.

Graeagle Lumber Company extended its railroad lines in the mid-1920s and purchased a new Baldwin locomotive. The new machine was so powerful that it could easily negotiate mountain grades of 6 percent and curves up to 32 degrees. Logs 4 and 5 feet in diameter were picked up at the landing and carried back to the millpond.

At the height of its operation in the 1930s, Graeagle Lumber Company employed between 300 and 350 men. At the mill itself were 155 to 185 men and another 150 to 200 worked in the woods.

A new sanitary stone dairy was erected near Denten Bridge during the 1930s. A new water system was installed and the roads were paved. Before the decade was over, gas or propane stoves began replacing wood stoves in the family homes. Electric stoves came by the early 1940s. Nearly every family had a radio to keep up with the news and provide listening enjoyment.

The Graeagle Fire Department sponsored social events during the mid-1930s. It managed the monthly Saturday night dances that became known as the Fireman's Ball. This good fellowship event was a part of Graeagle's social life for four decades, from the 1920s through the 1950s. Fire department sponsored family dinners and picnics were additional community events.

The first Graeagle fire engine was obtained in the mid-1930s by remodeling a company logging truck. Three or four fire hydrants, supplied by a 12-inch water main with a pressure of 100 pounds, were installed within the sawmill grounds to protect the entire lumberyard, mill, and factory buildings.

A U.S. Forest Service timber sale was obtained near Chilcoot and a good-sized camp was set up where the upper end of Frenchman Lake is now. To house the crew, the two-story bunkhouse No. 3 at Graeagle was disassembled and moved to Chilcoot. Cabins were erected for the married couples and a cookhouse and shop were built.

Logs were hauled by Sterling diesel trucks to the WPRR line at Chilcoot, loaded on flatcars by an old steam powered donkey engine and moved by rail to the Graeagle millpond. The lumber crew and mill hands in 1938 made 50¢ an hour for an eight-hour day. The only expense for the single men was the $1.25 a day for room and board. Each single man had a 10-by-12-foot room in one of the three bunkhouses and his bed was made every day. Sheets were cleaned twice a week. What more could a guy ask?

Married couples had it every bit as good: the monthly rent for their company homes, including water, electricity, and garbage, was $8.50, which gradually increased by the late 1940s to $12.50. Salaries had risen to $1.50 an hour by then. The monthly rent could be made in one working day.

Negative events began in 1951 when the millpond washed out. The cookhouse was shut down for good in 1954 because it was losing too much money. The paramount problem, however, was the reality that too many trees had been cut. Equally negative was the substitution of cardboard for wooden boxes.

140

The final tree was cut in September 1956 and the Graeagle Lumber mill shut down a month later on the last Saturday in October. Commemorating this memorable event, the mill's loud whistle was blown for five consecutive minutes at noon, signifying "that the last log had gone up the slip and through the band mill." Huge stacks of cut lumber still remained, of course; thus, the planing mill did not cease operations until May of the next year. When the final board went through the planing mill, lumber activity in the Mohawk Valley shut down.

Two hundred buyers from all over the western states came to a large auction the last week of May 1957 to purchase all the sawmill, box factory, and planing mill equipment. The final item sold at 9 p.m. The end of Graeagle's timber era was a reality. With the exception of two or three families, within a week of the auction, the town was deserted. All the other houses were vacant.

Harvey West Sr., a large timber operator in Placerville, offered California Fruit Exchange $450,000 in 1959 for the entire operation—$43 per acre, including improvements. They accepted. Property included in the purchase price was 10,482 acres of timberland, town, farm, and meadowland. The entire company town of Graeagle that West had purchased consisted of 42 houses, a clubhouse, store, butcher shop, dairy, warehouse, and school. Also included in the purchase price were the water and hydro power plant rights.

West asked Herb Roe and Lucy Vernazza and family to remain during this "semi-ghost town" transition period. Lucy well remembers walking down the once busy main street and seeing "only one light bulb burning in the entire town." Shirley West remembers her thoughts when she and her husband Harvey

This little donkey-powered cart was used to go around picking up trash in Graeagle around 1920. The cart is now on display at the Movin' West Trailer Park in Graeagle.

Jr. settled in Graeagle in 1959. Shirley felt she was coming to the "most isolated place in the world."

The Wests had plans, however. Graeagle's location was more accessible by the 1960s than it had been for the nineteenth-century sawmill owners and farmers. California now had automobiles, highways, and freeways, and Plumas County had paved roads.

Harvey West and sons formed the Graeagle Land and Water Company to manage their holdings. Pure mountain water was obtained from Long Lake high in the Lakes Basin. Harvey had the present-day Graeagle town segment of his property surveyed and divided into parcels measuring roughly one-third of an acre each. Sales were made beginning in 1960 for $1,995 to $3,500 per lot. Not wanting to move too fast, he decided to sell only 40 lots a year.

Townhouses and cluster homes were built beginning in 1974, 134 being completed by 1986. Graeagle Meadows Golf Course was constructed with the front nine holes being completed in 1968 and the back nine in 1970. Tennis courts were built in 1974.

Many of the company houses dating back to Arthur Davies and California Fruit Exchange days have been retained to the delight of those who appreciate the charm of an earlier period in our county history.

Ice from the pond on Grizzly Creek was shuttled to the ice deck at Portola, where refrigerator cars were loaded in approximately 2 minutes, 6 seconds per car. Crews were very competitive.

11. AMERICAN VALLEY: "THE GEM OF THE SIERRA"—QUINCY

In her 21st letter from *The Shirley Letters from the California Mines*, dating to October 1852, Dame Shirley wrote of Quincy, "The most beautiful spot that I ever saw in California."

The Turner brothers came to Plumas County in June 1850, looking for Gold Lake, but instead finding American Valley. They claimed all the lands lying south and east of Spanish Creek. Despite the valley's agricultural prospects, the Turner brothers were the only ones to establish permanent residence by 1851. In 1852, gold discoveries were made at Mill Creek and along the edges of American Valley and were worked with some success for years. Quartz operations were also worked on and off until the 1950s.

Negro Gulch was discovered on the site of today's Feather River College. A rich pay streak not more than a quarter-mile long and 500 feet wide was found by an African-American slave from Tennessee, who had come across the plains with the son of his former owner. Ground sluicing was employed by the twosome, who took out more than $30,000. Historian W.W. Kellogg described the location as "one of the richest paying pockets ever found."

Elizabethtown was an even richer find. Its location was 2 miles north of Quincy on the northwestern edge of American Valley. Elizabethtown's gold attracted an excited throng and, by 1853, was the most populous settlement in Plumas County.

H.J. Bradley purchased a portion of the Turner brothers' land during the summer of 1852. By fall, he erected a log building and public stopping house that he called the American Ranch. A historical marker in downtown Quincy designates the site. That same fall, Billy Houck, George Sharpe, and E.H. Pierce constructed a log saloon across the street from today's courthouse, catering to the numerous prospectors.

A large group of settlers arrived during late summer 1852 when Jim Beckwourth led a train of 17 wagons to the valley on their way west. Farmers arrived in 1852, such as Daniel Cate and E.W. Judkins, who founded the New England Ranch, William and son Russel Alford, who established what is now the Lee Ranch, and Mr. Goodrich from Illinois, who settled in 1851 on the Quincy-La Porte Road.

"Tune" Haun is shown here with a load of hay along the Meadow Valley Road. June was usually the height of haying season in these higher elevation valleys. In the background can be seen Quincy and some of its many business buildings as they looked in 1905.

He named his home the Illinois Ranch, later known as the Thompson, then Ramelli Ranch.

Along with E.W. Judkins and Joseph S. Boynton, Daniel Cate opened the first store and blacksmith shop in the valley and, during the 1852 and 1853 winter, erected the first sawmill along Mill Creek. Cate began a mule pack train business that operated for four years, bringing supplies from Marysville to Elizabethtown and to his ranch. He planted wheat on his New England Ranch in 1853 and built the first gristmill in the county in 1854. Cate was elected first county treasurer, but farming was his main love.

When the political conventions were held in the fall of 1852, Plumas County had not yet been formed. Plumas was a part of Butte County as established by the first state legislature in 1850. By 1853, there were discussions of the merits of splitting Butte County and forming a new county. Important issues included local administration, schools for children, crime protection, establishment of roads, and economic stability.

Lobbying in Sacramento by Plumas residents was successful. Plumas County was officially created by the state legislature on March 18, 1854. H.J. Bradley's American Ranch Hotel was designated as the provisional county seat until the fall elections when the people would vote and select a permanent location. Appointed to serve as Plumas County's organization commissioners were H.J. Bradley, Wilson S. Dean of Meadow Valley, and John W. Thompson of the Illinois Ranch. Between Plumas County's creation in March and the fall elections, H.J. Bradley laid out on paper the town he envisioned and named it Quincy in honor of his hometown of Quincy, Illinois.

Three locations vied for county seat: Elizabethtown, Quincy, and O'Neill's Flat, located between the two. As an inducement to the people to select Quincy, Bradley offered to donate land for a new courthouse if Quincy won the election.

A post office was established in 1855 and a small wooden jail erected. Construction of a toll road was begun from Quincy to Spanish Ranch in 1855. A livery stable was built and the Masonic Lodge went up that same year across the street from the present-day library. Colonel Calvin Rockwell built a 1-mile horse racetrack called Rockwell Park on the current Plumas County fairgrounds in 1856.

Elizabethtown went into decline by 1857, while Quincy's population was growing. Two schools were opened that year, one in Quincy and one in the valley to the east. A load of donated lumber and $375 were raised for construction of a school in the latter spot. Before long, the Pioneer School was erected and Sylvester A. Ballou was hired for $60 a month to teach the 19 children enrolled that year.

The *Old Mountaineer* was Quincy's first newspaper, operating from August 1855 until 1857, when it sold and became the *Plumas Argus*. Three newspapers were published in Quincy during the 1856 presidential election year. Pre-Civil War controversy was climaxing and the *Old Mountaineer,* the *Plumas Democrat,* and a new Republican Party paper, the *Fillmore Banner*, presented their sides of the controversy. The *Quincy Union* began its once-a-week service in 1865. The longest lasting paper, the *Plumas National,* started service in 1866. It later changed to *Plumas-National Bulletin,* then in 1931 to *Feather River Bulletin,* today's weekly.

In 1858, Reverend Philetus Grove was the first regularly assigned Methodist-Episcopalian pastor for Plumas County. Reverend Grove selected Quincy as his home as it was the most populous, family-type settlement in the county, with a population of about 200 people.

There was no church in Quincy or anywhere else in the county. The entire county was Reverend Grove's parish. He traveled the region, conducting religious services at homes, in halls, wherever he could get worshipers together. In Quincy, he used the courthouse for worship service. Later, the Exchange Saloon was purchased by the county for a town hall, Sunday school, and until 1875, a church.

The first county courthouse was built in 1859; the public square where it was built was donated by H.J. Bradley, Joseph Green, and George W. Sharpe. The town's first drugstore was erected that same year, followed by the Coburn House Hotel. Edwards Meat Market purchased a handsome Concord-built butcher wagon for home shopping. Buck Whiting's dog sled arrived in Quincy once a week during the winter with mail. The first legal hangings were carried out in 1859 at Hangman's Ravine, next to the original cemetery. A new brick jail was built in 1863 for $7,035.

John and William Clinch came to the United States from England in 1854 to mine gold. In 1855, they struck pay dirt at Sawpit Flat, sent for their wives, and continued mining and living at Sawpit until 1872. Trading mining and Sawpit Flat's cold snowy winters for farming, they moved to their American Valley ranch just north of Quincy, which they had purchased in 1857. Within a decade, their ranch became a county showplace where they raised wheat, vegetables, and cattle. Livestock from their ranch supplied the Clinch Meat Market across from the Town Hall Theater in downtown Quincy. Their Sears & Roebuck mail order cement-block house was built in the second decade of the twentieth century for $2,000 and is located at the corner of Quincy Junction and Lee Road.

B.F. Chandler came from New York to settle in American Valley in 1873. Chandler developed a 440-acre tract consisting of timber and farmlands producing hay, grain, cattle, apples, and 60 acres of vegetables. As the years progressed, he built an elegant brick residence on Chandler Road that is still standing. During one year, he cut 300 tons of clover and timothy hay, grew 80,000 pounds of cabbage per acre, 60,000 pounds of beets, 60,000 pounds of carrots, and other vegetables in proportion. Chandler's apple orchard produced 300 to 500 boxes of apples yearly.

Allen J. Welden established a 300-acre ranch in 1855 along Mill Creek where the Sierra Pacific Industries plant is now located. His house and the many barns stood until the mid-1990s when the mill demolished them. The old Bell Ranch is also occupied by Sierra Pacific Industries. Nearby, J.H. Yeates had a large ranch that later became the site of the Cedar Mill, Essex Mill, then Siskiyou-Plumas Mill, and now Wilburn Construction.

The Plumas House was erected in 1853 as a log hotel opposite today's courthouse, but burned in 1863. It was rebuilt in 1866 and featured a large parlor, dining room, hall, kitchen, pantry, and barroom. Thirty bedrooms and a spring floor ballroom were upstairs. It was added to still more in the 1870s and was a favorite for over 50 years, having "a reputation among travelers and tourists as being one of the very best hotels in the mountains." Electric lighting and a heating plant were installed in 1910. During the 1910s, most major social functions in town were held at the Plumas House. Hot and cold running water were added in 1918. Fire burned everything down in 1923.

Hotel Quincy was built on the same site in 1925, sporting 50 guest rooms, steam heat, electric lights, telephones, and a 28-by-40-foot dining room. For more than three decades, it was "the place" in Quincy. Fire destroyed it in November 1966.

Because of the hydraulic mines and heavy capital being poured into the county's mines, the 1870s was the most economically lucrative decade for Quincy. The Town Hall Theater was erected in 1872. Activity swelled in 1874 when new telegraph lines reached Quincy from San Francisco. A new brewery opened that same year, augmenting the first-class Capital, Courthouse, and Pony saloons.

Saloon activity to some would equate violence and disorder rather than law and order. It wasn't the case in Quincy, however, for as a visiting newspaper reporter commented, the town has a "good courthouse and jail, but the latter we are assured, is frequently for months without a tenant."

The first hospital in Quincy was located on Beskeen Lane near the old county cemetery. The make-up of this first hospital was three cabins placed end to end. It was a reasonably self-sufficient hospital, as the superintendent spent much of the time growing vegetables and grain or milking cows and raising cattle. In 1880, a new hospital was built to replace the existing one.

Response to growing concerns over fire protection was met when Quincy Hose Company No. 1, the forerunner of today's Quincy Volunteer Fire Department, was organized. Their building stood just east of the present Town Hall Theater and then was later moved directly across Main Street.

The surge of new residents meant many school children. The Masonic Lodge, having served as the town school site since 1857, became too crowded. Responding to the need, school trustees approved a $3,500 bid in July 1876 to build a permanent school. Two months later, a 33-by-50-foot, two-story brick school was built on Church Street near the Methodist church. Each schoolroom was 30 by 38 feet with 10-foot anterooms on each floor. A cupola with a bell completed the structure. Sixty-three students showed up for classes when the school year opened in mid-September.

Lyceum meetings were held weekly at the Town Hall to satisfy literary desires. Women's suffrage, capital punishment, and transportation were among the topics of interest. Two sides, composed of three knowledgeable men on each side, debated the issues.

Because of the great distance between Quincy proper and the outlying ranches of American Valley, the Pioneer School was built in 1857 to serve those families. This building remained in operation until 1974 when it was moved to the Plumas County Fairgrounds for display.

Cakewalks, the popular new game of baseball, musical entertainment by the town brass band, literary societies, dances, circuses, and the county fair became the social activities to lighten the normal 12-hour workdays. Also available as diversions, but not by all, were boxing matches, horse races, bull and bear fights, and cock fights.

As the primary supply town for the surrounding mines, Quincy's population had grown to about 1,000 people during the 1870s. Gold was the cornerstone for Quincy's prosperity and when the Anti-Debris Act was passed in 1884, curtailing hydraulic mining, business activity substantially declined, and a great many people were forced to leave the area.

In 1889, the Quincy Electric Light and Power Company began using Gansner Creek water and a Pelton Wheel to provide hydropower for some of Quincy's residents. By April 1900, the Quincy Electric Light and Power Company was able to announce it was "now prepared to furnish lights for residences and business houses at moderate rates."

By 1901, Quincy also had eight fire hydrants. Two years later, the Plumas County Bank, the town's first, began operations with a capital stock of $25,000. A new bank building, which stands today, was erected at the corner of Main and Harbison Streets.

Dr. Bert James Laswell arrived, serving as American Valley's doctor for nearly four decades. "Doc" Laswell immediately established himself as the respected and trusted family doctor, reaching patients by horseback, horse-drawn buggy, skis, or

The winter of 1889–1890 saw a particularly heavy snowfall. A number of Quincy townspeople turned out for this photo to emphasize how deep the snow was. This view is from the Plumas House Hotel east up Main Street.

on foot. A new hospital was erected in 1915 at the present-day site of the Plumas County Courthouse Annex. It was a 45-by-117-foot two-story brick building containing 12 bedrooms, 2 large multi-bed wards, and an operating room.

In 1908, Plumas County High School was formed and, after two years at a temporary facility in Greenville, the school was transferred to Quincy in 1912. In 1914, a new first class high school was constructed on China Rock, once Quincy's Chinatown, above where today's high school is located. Students from all over the county attended the Plumas County High School, lodging in Quincy with relatives and friends or renting a room from town residents. In 1905, a handsome K-8 school was built on Church Street to replace the structurally failing 1876 brick building. Finished at a cost of $8,698, the attractive structure boasted all the modern conveniences. That building, with additions and remodeling, served until 1951, when it was converted into Plumas Unified School District administrative offices.

Radios hadn't made their appearance in Quincy in 1918, so the town learned of the end of World War I by Western Union telegraph. Within ten minutes, everyone was outside shouting and celebrating. The church bell began ringing. The Quincy Hose Cart bell joined in, followed by the blasting of the lumber mill whistle. Atop its fire station tower on Main Street in the next block east of the courthouse, the fire bell pealed enthusiastically. Jack Wilson rounded up the Quincy Brass Band and, moving to the bandstand on the courthouse lawn, gave a spirited musical performance. A parade was formed, and participants cheerfully joined hands and began marching down Main Street.

With the war's end, normalcy resumed; it was a time to plan for the future, a time to consider economic growth for Quincy. Gold mining activity had declined in the Quincy-Meadow Valley region, but the lumber industry was beginning its commercial emergence. F.S. Murphy built a large sawmill at the eastern edge of Quincy in 1913. Quincy Railroad Company provided the mill with a spur track for shipment to Quincy Junction and the WPRR.

WPRR and the lumber industry provided major employment opportunities to Quincy and Plumas County during 60 years following the rail line's completion in 1910. Keddie was an important location where scores of jobs were offered for engineers, firemen, brakemen, conductors, yardmen, and field crews.

The cornerstone of the present Plumas County Courthouse was laid in 1919. Two years of construction followed, the elegant building being finished in 1921, with Governor William Stephens participating in the September dedication ceremonies. Its graceful 33-by-55-foot foyer and 36-foot ceiling, Ionic columns, and marble facings in the corridor create a splendid impression. Marble stairs surmounted by iron railings and oak window casings all add to the courthouse's beauty and stateliness.

Plumas County's first free library opened in Quincy in 1915. The Masonic Lodge became the first home for the library's collection of over 1,400 books. The first motion pictures were shown at the Town Hall Theater in 1910 or 1911. Once the new courthouse was completed, the library was moved into it in 1921, where it remained for over 50 years until a new library was erected. A memorial room was instituted in the new building also, moving next to the courthouse lobby; then in 1968 into its own new structure.

During the 1920s, a private, industrial hospital catering to loggers, sawmill workers, and ranchers suffering on-the-job accidents was established at the J.D. Goodwin residence on the corner of Jackson and Buchanan Streets. In addition, since no local or nearby hospitals delivered babies until the 1930s, Dr. Laswell convinced Verbenia Moseley and her husband to convert their home into quarters where pregnant women could give birth to their babies and remain under care until they were able to return home. So successful was the Beno Maternity Home that it remained in business for more than a decade, from 1927 until just before World War II began in 1941.

By the end of the 1920s, street signs were put along Main Street. In 1928, two and a half blocks of Main Street became the first hard-surfaced road in the county. Cement was laid from the new Hotel Quincy at Main and Court Streets to Fillmore Street.

1933 was a milestone year for Quincy and its concern for fire protection, for the town's first fire engine was purchased that year. It was a brand new, white, 1.5-ton Dodge with 750 feet of fire hose that could pump 350 gallons a minute from suction or 400 gallons from a fire hydrant.

Its acquisition was none too soon, for half of downtown Quincy burned down on Wednesday, August 28, 1934. The fire originated in the basement of the three-story Grand Central Hotel on Main Street across from the courthouse. The fire engine rushed from its station a mere half block away to Lawrence Street where a hydrant was located. Hoses were quickly connected and the water-versus-fire battle begun, but it was too late, as the hotel was a "seething mass of flames."

Volunteers moved stock and fixtures from places of business on Main Street to the courthouse lawn. Heavy winds fanned the flames eastward with appalling rapidity. They jumped across Bradley Street to continue onto other business buildings. People standing in the courthouse entrance "were scorched by the intense heat."

Quincy's fire department crew was assisted by every able-bodied man in town, plus a crew of CCC men. Despite their valiant help, the conflagration relentlessly drove them back as the flames spread both east and west on Main Street and north towards Lawrence Street "until it appeared the entire business district, and possibly the rest of Quincy was fated to be destroyed."

The roaring blaze soon gutted the Quincy Drug Store, its brick front wall collapsing into the street. By now, the fire along Main Street's business district was engulfing much of two city blocks. Quincy's total downtown destruction was prevented when Portola and Greenville fire department crews and their fire engines arrived in only 40 minutes after receiving urgent calls for assistance. As they were reaching town, Red Savage, using a big county tractor, yanked a one-story Chinese restaurant into the street to create a firebreak and stop the spread of the flames.

By evening, the town's reservoirs were almost exhausted. The Quincy Fire Department had lost 800 feet of hose, leaving only 1,000 feet in serviceable condition. Fourteen business structures, warehouses, a rooming house, and Joe Yien's home were destroyed. While there was $176,000 in damage, no one was killed or seriously injured. Quincy's devastating fire was a severe blow to the community, but buildings were quickly rebuilt over the next several years.

A second town fire truck was purchased in 1938 and a new fire station built in 1939 on Lawrence Street and Railway Avenue. Sawmill owner C.A. King furnished the lumber at cost. The town's first ambulance, acquired the year before, was housed and manned by the firemen.

A town airport was laid out in 1933 off Bucks Lake Road, where the Bellamy housing tract is now located, and the town's first golf course was busy. The Town Hall Theater, burned in 1934, was rebuilt in 1936. A Catholic church was built in 1929. Seven feet of snow and a big flood disrupted the valley in 1937, but a momentous event of long lasting importance happened that same year. The Feather River Canyon Highway was finished, allowing easy, comfortable automobile travel.

When the Great Depression began in the early 1930s, East Quincy was still nothing more than a quiet meadowland portion of American Valley, with cattle ranchers, hay and grain fields, and vegetable gardens. Lee, Vierra, Welden,

Flood cycles vary in Plumas County, but the winter of 1893 was one of the wettest, although no permanent property damage was recorded. Travel was hindered, a few bridges went out, but mostly it gave the photographer something to record. This view is from the old courthouse north toward Spanish Creek.

Horse racing has been a perennial California favorite, and Plumas County is no exception. Colonel Rockwell established a race track on the present fairgrounds, known as Rockwell Park, to accommodate the sport. This photo was taken c. 1890.

Graham, and Shipe ranches were well-known names at that time. A saloon called the Stone House was built as the 1930s moved into the 1940s, catering to local residents, sportsmen, and ranch workers. No stores or other business establishments existed in East Quincy. A two-lane dirt road went over Cemetery Hill. Property demand was almost nonexistent, 12 acres selling for $250 in 1936, 1 acre for $25 in 1942.

The 1940s meant World War II and an explosive change for East Quincy. In 1941, Harry Lee subdivided his ranch and others soon followed. By the end of the war, houses sprang up and people moved in. By spring 1946, the *Feather River Bulletin* reported East Quincy to be "the fastest growing area in Plumas County." A new firehouse soon followed. By 1955, East Quincy, with a population of 3,500, had more residents than 101-year-old "Main Quincy." Since the end of the war, more than 100 new homes had been built and among the new businesses were Jack Boyd's large grocery store and Mansell's Mercury automobile agency. By the mid-1950s, the local newspaper boasted "American Valley is the youngest and fastest growing community in northeastern California."

The World War II years were a time of anxiety for everyone, especially the parents of the many young men overseas. Food and gasoline rationing, air raid practices, and a general "belt tightening" became a new way of life. The Plumas County Bank closed its doors in 1941 and several business shops followed. On the positive side, American Valley resident and Quincy High School graduate William

"Billy" Clinch made a name for himself when he wrote the Air Force anthem: "Off we go into the wild, blue yonder, climbing high into the sun . . . "

A Quonset hut Veterans Hall was built in 1946 and seasonal Greyhound Bus service began the same year. Nellie Gansner gave Plumas County 103 acres of land on the outskirts of Quincy for a county airport. Construction of the airport began in May 1949, and the 3,100-foot-long by 75-foot-wide runway was finished by Thanksgiving of that year.

In 1947, Tulsa Scott was appointed to the position of manager of the Plumas County Fair. Green lawns and thousands of blooming petunias soon earned the Plumas County Fairgrounds the title of "The Cleanest and Greenest in the West." Carnival entertainment, exhibits, a rodeo, professional singers, hotdog and popcorn booths, and the Pacific Coast Logging Championship were among the activities of the Plumas County Fair.

Gansner Park was created in 1951 on land donated by Mr. and Mrs. F.B. Gansner. That same year, a brand new, modern, earthquake safe elementary school was built on Alder Street, replacing the one built on Church Street in 1905. The new Quincy Junior-Senior High School was finished in 1953. In 1952 the sealing and paving of Quincy's streets eliminated dust and mud.

Impressive as all this progress was, nature decided to reveal her might. A more powerful than normal deluge of rain and snow occurred during the winter of 1951 and 1952; before it was over, Quincy's downtown Main Street had received 7 feet of snow. In January 1953, American Valley became "one vast lake" as a result of heavy rains, the resulting flood washing away the bridge at the Spanish Creek-Spring Garden Creek junction.

In East Quincy, an 80-by-140-foot National Guard Armory was built in 1955 and a remodeled East High Street home became the Lutheran church in 1956. Quincy Community Television Association was awarded a television franchise in 1963. Cable television followed and all the major networks could be received with perfect clarity. Dial telephones finally replaced the old-time manual switchboards in 1967.

Longtime Quincy resident Stella Fay Miller passed away in 1964 and bequeathed $152,000 to build the Plumas County Museum, her bequest becoming a reality when the structure was erected on the corner of Coburn and Jackson Streets in 1968.

Higher education came to Quincy and Plumas County in 1968 when Feather River College was established. Its initial classrooms were located at the fairgrounds, then at the National Guard Armory. In 1971, a permanent 160-acre campus was constructed on the old Meylert Ranch, west of Quincy.

Heavy rains in 1963 caused Spanish Creek floodwaters to wash out the Highway 70/89 bridge at the north end of town. In 1972, a new $280,000 library opened in downtown Quincy. A modern jail was built in East Quincy in 1976, replacing the one located on the fourth floor of the courthouse. Pioneer School, the first schoolhouse built in Plumas County in 1857 and used continuously for 117 years, was moved to the Plumas County Fairgrounds to retire in 1974.

A shopping center with a dozen stores in a single location was built in 1976 where the large F.S. Murphy and Quincy Lumber Company sawmill and log decks had been located. Ten sawmills have closed since the beginning of World War II. Sierra Pacific is the only sawmill still operating in Quincy at the turn of the twenty-first century. It cuts more board feet annually than all the Quincy mills put together and employs 175 to 200 people.

Quincy and its surroundings have often been referred to as "the Gem of the Sierra." Quincy prefers its small-town atmosphere, refusing to become an incorporated city, yet still maintains its distinguished position as the "county seat."

As Plumas County embarks on its second 150 years, it will be with pride in our past and faith in our future. It is hoped that in another 150 years, when some future historian is writing another history of Plumas County, this book will be a foundation for that work.

In August of 1934 a fire erupted from a small laundry in back of the Grand Central Hotel, now the site of Ayoob's Department Store. It quickly engulfed that building and spread east as far as the Town Hall Theater, which it also consumed. Fire trucks from other communities responded to assist Quincy. No one was hurt, and a new business section arose from the ashes.

BIBLIOGRAPHY

BOOKS, DIARIES, AND PUBLICATIONS

Beckwourth, James P. with Thomas D. Bonner. *The Life and Adventures of James P. Beckwourth.* New York: Alfred A. Knopf, 1931.

Bibliography of Early California Forestry. United States Forest Service, California Forest and Range Experiment Station with assistance by Works Progress Administration, 1939–1941.

Bibliography of Early California Forestry. California State Board of Forestry, 1888.

Billington, Ray Allen. *The Far Western Frontier.* New York: Harper and Row, 1956.

Browne, J. Ross. *Report of J. Ross Browne on the Mineral Resources of the States and Territories West of the Rocky Mountains.* Washington, D.C.: U.S. Government Printing Office, 1868.

Coleman, Charles M. *P.G. & E. of California.* New York: McGraw-Hill Book Company, 1952.

Dixon, Roland B. *The Northern Maidu.* New York: Bulletin of the American Museum of Natural History, 1905.

Downie, Major William. *Hunting for Gold, Reminiscences of Personal Experience and Research in the Early Days of the Pacific Coast from Alaska to Panama.* San Francisco: California Publishing Co, 1893.

Fariss and Smith. *The Illustrated History of Plumas, Lassen, and Sierra Counties.* San Francisco: Howell-North, 1882.

Fowler, Stephen and James. *Journal of Stephen L. & James E. Fowler, June 15, 1850.* Bancroft Library, Berkeley, CA.

Frickstad, Walter N. "A Century of California Post Offices, 1848-1954." Oakland, CA: A Philatelic Research Society publication, 1955.

Giffen, Helen, ed., *The Diaries of Peter Decker.* Georgetown, CA: Talisman Press, 1966.

Gould, Helen W. *La Porte Scrapbook.* La Porte, CA: Self published, 1972.

Guinn, J.M. *History of the State of California.* Chicago: Chapman Publishing Company, 1906.

Hall, Jacqueline and JoEllen. *Italian-Swiss Settlement in Plumas County, 1860 to 1920.* Chico: Association for Northern California Records and Research, 1973.

Hanft, Robert M. *Red River, Paul Bunyan's Own Lumber Company and Its Railroad.* Chico: California State University, Chico, 1979.

Heizer, Robert F. *Handbook of North American Indians.* Washington, D.C.: Smithsonian Institution, 1978.

Holliday, J.S. *The World Rushed In.* New York: Simon and Schuster, 1981.

Hutchinson, W.H. *California, the Golden Shore by the Sundown Sea.* Belmont, CA: Star Publishing Company, 1980.

———. *California Heritage, A History of Northern California Lumbering.* Diamond National Corporation: Chico State University, Chico, CA, 1974.

Jones, William Allen. Master's thesis. California State University, Chico, 1966.

Lawson, Scott. *The Giant's Roar, A History of Badger Hill Mine.* Quincy: Self published, 1993.

McIlhaney, Edward W. *Recollections of a '49er.* Kansas City, MO: Hailman Miller Printing Company, 1908.

Oglesby, Richard, ed. *The Shirley Letters from the California Mines.* Salt Lake City: Peregrine Smith, Inc., 1970.

Parke, Charles B. *Diary, June 18-26, 1850.* Huntington Library, San Marino, CA.

Parker, William Tell. *Diary, November 17-29, 1850.* Huntington Library, San Marino, CA.

Pricer, Barbara. *The Chinese in Northern California.* Quincey, CA: Forest Printing, 1996.

Puter, Steven A. D. and Horace Stevens. *Looters of the Public Domain.* Portland, OR: Portland Printing House, 1908.

Read, Georgia Willis and Ruth Gaines, ed. *The Journals, Drawings, and Other Papers of J. Goldsborough Bruff.* New York: Columbia Publishing, 1949.

Tung, William. *The Chinese In America, 1820-1973.* Dobbs Ferry, NY: Oceana Publications, Inc., 1974.

Warren, Judith Ann. Master's thesis. University of California, Berkeley, 1968.

Windeler, Augustus and W. Turrentine Jackson, ed. *The California Gold Rush Diary of a German Sailor.* Berkeley: Howell North Books, 1969.

Young, Jim. *History of Rich Bar.* Quincy: Self published, 1983.

Newspapers and Periodicals

The Blue Anchor. California Fruit Exchange magazine, December 1934.

Greenville Bulletin. Greenville, California.

Indian Valley Record. Greenville, California.

Marysville Herald. Marysville, California.

Marysville Placer Times. Marysville, California.

Pacific Logging Congress Proceedings. Forestry Library University of California, Berkeley.

Plumas Independent. Quincy, California.

Plumas National. Quincy, California.

Plumas National-Bulletin. Quincy, California.

Portola Reporter. Portola, California.
Reno Evening Gazette and Stockman. Reno, Nevada.
Reno Evening Gazette. Reno, Nevada.
Sacramento Bee. Sacramento, California.
The Timberman.
West Coast Lumberman.

Files and Bulletins

Accordion photograph files. Indian Valley Museum, Taylorsville, CA.
William T. Ballou folder. Bancroft Library, Berkeley, CA.
California Journal of Mines and Geology. California State Printing Office: April 1937.
California Legislative Assembly Journals, Appendix 3, 1894.
Dunn, Mary. *Scrapbook*, Plumas County Museum.
Gopher Hill folder. Plumas County Museum.
Lawry, Helen Hall. *Scrapbook*, Plumas County Museum.
Minutes book, 1855, Plumas County Board of Supervisors. Plumas County Clerk, Quincy, California
Plumas County Assessment Rolls, Plumas County Museum, Quincy, California.
Plumas County Historical Society, various volumes, 1-66.
Plumas County Resolutions. Courtesy of Francis O'Rourke, former Plumas County Road Department Commissioner.
Plumas Eureka Mine folder. Plumas County Museum
Plumas Mining & Water Company folder. Plumas County Museum.
Sierra County Historical Society. *Quarterly issue,* June 10, 1969.
Simpson, Vic. Article in *Red River folder,* Plumas County Museum.
State Resources, Vol. IV, Nos. 3 and 4. California State Printing Office.
Weaverville Joss House folder. State of California, The Resources Agency.
Western Pacific Railroad folder. Plumas County Museum.
Whiting Family folder. Plumas County Museum.

Personal Interviews

Beatty, William M.
Bellows, Jack.
Cotter, George.
Cooke, Bob.
Donnenwirth, Dorothy.
Fonda, Uldene.
Hunt, Elmore.
Hunter, Jack and Pearl.
Johnson, Jim.
Leonhardt, Ernest.
Malvich, Marian.

Mason, Buster.
Meyers, Orvall.
Moon, Robert Gee.
Striplin, Joe.
Thieler, Al.
Valverde, Andrew.
Watkins, Duke.
Way, Glen.
West, Harvey.

INDEX